MURDER ON THE OHIO BELLE

MURDER
ON THE
OHIO BELLE

Stuart W. Sanders

K UNIVERSITY PRESS OF KENTUCKY

Copyright © 2020 by The University Press of Kentucky

Scholarly publisher for the Commonwealth,
serving Bellarmine University, Berea College, Centre
College of Kentucky, Eastern Kentucky University,
The Filson Historical Society, Georgetown College,
Kentucky Historical Society, Kentucky State University,
Morehead State University, Murray State University,
Northern Kentucky University, Transylvania University,
University of Kentucky, University of Louisville,
and Western Kentucky University.
All rights reserved.

Editorial and Sales Offices: The University Press of Kentucky
663 South Limestone Street, Lexington, Kentucky 40508-4008
www.kentuckypress.com

Unless otherwise noted, photographs are courtesy of the Library of Congress.

Cataloging-in-Publication data is available from the Library of Congress.

ISBN 978-0-8131-7871-4 (hardcover : alk. paper)
ISBN 978-0-8131-7873-8 (epub)
ISBN 978-0-8131-7872-1 (pdf)

This book is printed on acid-free paper meeting
the requirements of the American National Standard
for Permanence in Paper for Printed Library Materials.

∞

Manufactured in the United States of America.

Member of the Association
of University Presses

Contents

Introduction

On April 5, 1856, the *Shepherdstown Register*, a newspaper located in what is now West Virginia, ran a story about a murder that took place on the Mississippi River. "The details are truly awful," the reporter stated, "and well calculated to cause a thrill of horror."[1]

Although Shepherdstown stands on the Potomac River across from Maryland, readers were captivated by this killing that took place more than seven hundred miles away. They viewed western waters—the Ohio and Mississippi Rivers—as mysterious places of conflict. This murder, and the "thrill of horror" it caused, surely reinforced that vision.

The genesis of that reporter's revulsion was the discovery of a drowned man found bobbing in the water, his legs and arms tied to a chair. In addition to capturing the attention of editors across the nation, his death pushed authorities to ask a number of questions: Who was he? What had happened that led to his horrific demise? Why had he been bound and tossed into the river to suffer? When I began researching this story, I asked similar questions. I also wondered about the broader implications of this murder that had been reported about across the country.

The dead man was a Mississippian who had been a passenger on the Cincinnati-based steamboat the *Ohio Belle*. At first it appeared that his brutal end was a simple story of southern honor culture gone awry—a tale of murder and vengeance. I soon found, however, that the life of this drowned man—and the history of the *Ohio Belle*—told a more complex tale about deep tensions found within antebellum America.

1

A fascinating cast of characters revealed these strains in the cultural fabric: the drowned man, whose true identity and violent past was uncovered only after he was retrieved from the river; the steamboat clerk Hiram Stevens, killed in a flash of honor-fueled vengeance; John Sebastian, the captain of the *Ohio Belle*, a cool-headed river man who later lost his arm while piloting a Union gunboat; the famed actress Matilda Heron, who temporarily saved a killer from the wrath of an angry mob; and finally, the steamboat itself, the *Ohio Belle*, which ran passengers and freight from Cincinnati to New Orleans before being captured by a ragtag band of Arkansas secessionists.

The history of the *Ohio Belle* helps us better understand nineteenth-century riverine culture. It also illustrates deeper national issues of consequence. How, for example, did Americans contend with western rivers that were the borderland between the enslaved and free? How did they deal with fugitive slaves and respond to interpersonal violence and vigilante justice? How did they wrestle with cultural differences, including the strain between those who followed a regional, gendered, and racialized code of honor and those who did not? The history of this steamboat also demonstrates the struggle with class prejudice and the influence of wealth and status on public opinion and media coverage. Moreover, as the most momentous of these issues—slavery—split the nation apart, the *Ohio Belle* also explains how Northern-owned boats and their passengers and crew fared on Southern waters during the secession crisis and the Civil War.

The Ohio and Mississippi Rivers drove to the heart of many of these issues. Dividing geographically, politically, and philosophically a nation at odds with itself, these waters brought travelers from across the nation together to ride the border between slavery and freedom. Many of those passengers, including Alexis de Tocqueville, saw firsthand that the river was more than a physical barrier as the economic consequences of slavery were evident. Furthermore, the rivers showcased the tension between the old United States and the expanding west as steamboats like the *Ohio Belle* pushed the nation to grow and change.

This vessel also demonstrates the fluidity of that river border. The *Belle* and other northern-owned steamboats transported enslaved people, and profited from the peculiar institution. In one instance, the *Belle* carried an enslaved man to Cincinnati and became involved in a fugitive slave case, thereby demonstrating both the economic and political consequences of operating along the Ohio River. In addition, at a time when class differences were sharp, steamboats like the *Ohio Belle* were great equalizers along that border, bringing together members of the southern planter gentry, famous actresses, merchants, and travelers of the more middling class. This led to a mingling of cultural differences that could have grim consequences. In 1856, for example, crew members on the *Ohio Belle* refused to acknowledge one traveler's claim to honor after he murdered one of their own.

This incident and others along the river reveal a major tension in antebellum society: how Americans contended with violence, including homicide, lynching, slavery, accidental death, and warfare. Passengers and crew sometimes traveled with an unsavory lot, including gamblers, thieves, con artists, and those whom Kentucky attorney Ben Hardin once called "the bowie knife and pistol gentry." Those of this type were armed, white, southern men who were primed to take affront and were prepared to kill in order to protect their manhood and reputation. Often acquitted of murder thanks to dubious claims of self-defense, they made violence appear to be an acceptable form of conflict resolution. Less than a decade after the *Ohio Belle* stopped traveling western waters, for example, a journalist covering a Bluegrass State murder trial wrote, "Human life is held to-day more cheaply than ever before. Courts and juries too often wink at crime, and on the rising generation we seem to be fostering an array of young 'bloods' whose chief reliance for future honors is on the pistol and the bowie knife."[2] Thanks to this ilk, those who rode aboard the *Ohio Belle* were familiar with concealed weapons and their deadly application. They were also acquainted with other forms of violence, including murder and vengeance, the brutalization of the enslaved, steamboat disasters, the drowning of passengers and crew, and toward the end of the *Belle*'s history, depredations committed by Civil War guerrillas. For these travelers, the risk of violence and danger was ever present. Therefore, the story of the *Ohio Belle*—from when the first vessel to bear that name cast off in 1839 until the third *Belle* was sold for scrap after the Civil War—provides insight into how Americans applied and reacted to violence along these borderland rivers.

The history of the *Ohio Belle* also presents a portrait of how western antebellum society embraced retribution. Although many hoped for justice when a wrong had been perpetrated, the threat of vengeance loomed ever present. Whether it was vigilantism on board the *Ohio Belle,* Union troops burning a Tennessee town in revenge for irregular violence, or a steamboat captain hoping to retaliate for his lost vessel, the history of the *Belle* illuminates society's desire for reprisal. The need for a violent reckoning was, for many, a viable and popular solution. Mobs pulled slaves from jails and hanged them; rioters threw rocks and brickbats, and burned jurors and lawyers in effigy; riverboat crew members beat and shaved the heads of thieves who robbed passengers. And, in a rare example of common folk meting out vigilante justice on a member of the southern gentry, in 1856 a man was tied to a chair and dumped into the Mississippi River to drown.

This study, therefore, considers these tensions—interpersonal violence, slavery, honor culture, and retribution—through the lens of the *Ohio Belle*. Chapter 1 examines the importance of the Ohio River, the risks of steamboat travel, and the way that these vessels disrupted the economy on western waters. Chapters 2 and 3 discuss an important fugitive slave case involving the *Ohio Belle* and the murder that took place on board the vessel in 1856. Chapter 4 surveys violence on the Ohio and Mississippi Rivers and examines honor culture. Chapter 5 notes the consequences of the murder of the boat's clerk, Hiram Stevens, and the perpetration of mob rule and vigilante justice in the Ohio River Valley. Chapter 6 looks at how class prejudice influenced the reporting of Stevens's murder and reveals the killer's true identity. Chapter 7 examines how Northern-owned boats fared as they traded on Southern waters during the secession crisis, and explores the *Ohio Belle*'s Civil War service and that of its captain, John Sebastian. Finally, chapter 8 reveals what ultimately happened to the passengers and crew who were present during the 1856 murder. It also outlines the final days of that "splendid passenger steamer," the *Ohio Belle*.[3]

Writing this book—and reconstructing the vessel's history for the first time—strengthened my resolve that a single event, including a forgotten murder on a nineteenth-century steamboat, can illuminate a more important, broader narrative about our past. In this instance, the *Ohio Belle* teaches us about important themes from the nineteenth century that are still relevant today. Honor killings still exist around the world. Vigilantes still believe themselves to be above the law. Injustice rooted in race, religion, and class affects our communities. Regional differences and social prejudices still divide us. Wealth influences media coverage. History, including the tale of a murder on a steamboat, still matters.

1

A Splendid New Boat

On March 14, 1856, the side-wheeled steamboat *Ohio Belle* pulled up to the wharf at Smithland, Kentucky, to pick up goods and passengers. There, nearly one thousand people had built their lives where the Cumberland River meets the Ohio. The previous day, the *Belle* had stopped at Evansville, Indiana, to unload freight before continuing on to the Mississippi River. At Evansville, a reporter wrote, the *Belle* was "very heavily laden, and with a great many passengers on board, including Miss Heron, the eminent actress, and her troupe." The boat was abuzz with talk about that actress, Matilda Heron, who had earned renown as the lead role in *Camille,* an Alexandre Dumas play that Heron had translated and performed up and down the rivers. It was a tragic love story involving a courtesan dying from tuberculosis, and Heron played the part with emotional dexterity and depth.[1]

Smithland, located just upriver from Paducah, Kentucky, was a frequent stopping point on the Ohio River. In 1841, Edward Jarvis, a passenger on the steamboat *Edward Shippen*, recalled that "Smithland is built of brick and wood and in genteel and shabby style intermingled to suit all tastes; the streets look exceedingly muddy." In the years that followed, the town had not changed drastically. On that March day in 1856, when an aristocratic Mississippian named J. B. Jones boarded the *Ohio Belle* at Smithland, he likely sneered at the town before scraping the mud off his boots and boarding the vessel. Sixteen years later, another passenger remembered Jones's appearance on the *Belle*. "When the steamer arrived . . . there came on board a man who was evidently recovering from a drinking spree. His clothes were of good material and fitted him well, tho' somewhat impaired by use. His face was soiled, and his beard had grown to an uncomely length. His eyes were bloodshot and glared unnaturally. His linen needed a change." Jones was rumpled, had a highborn swagger, and appeared to be intoxicated. When he lurched on board, he presented himself as a southern gentleman of means.[2]

Jones, Heron, and the other passengers on the *Belle* were enduring a sharp run of cold weather. In the weeks before their voyage, an "ice bridge" across the Ohio River had closed the river for fifty-three days. On February 25, the ice finally cracked, allowing boats to traverse the water. By mid-March, when the *Belle* docked at Smithland, the Ohio River was falling, and it was snowing sporadically.[3]

Passengers and crew traveling on other steamboats, flatboats, keelboats, and ferries would have recognized the name that adorned that side-wheel steamer. At least three steamboats named the *Ohio Belle* had plied the Cincinnati to New Orleans trade route since the late 1830s, with one boat replacing the other. Constructed in 1839, 1843, and 1855, respectively, each successive *Ohio Belle* grew in tonnage—from 294 tons to 310 tons to 406 tons in 1855—as river passage became more important to the growth of the nation.[4]

The Ohio River was integral to that growth. Formed at Pittsburgh, Pennsylvania, where the Allegheny and Monongahela Rivers converge, the Ohio River runs nearly one thousand miles to the Mississippi River at Cairo, Illinois. The river carves out the borders of West Virginia, Kentucky, Illinois, Indiana, and Ohio, and is fed by multiple tributaries, including the Kanawha, Kentucky, Wabash, Cumberland, Tennessee, and other rivers. Running from three hundred to six hundred yards wide, in 1856, the time when J. B. Jones boarded the steamboat, it spanned nearly six hundred yards at Cincinnati, the home of the *Ohio Belle*.[5]

That year, the river's majesty was described by James T. Lloyd, a chronicler of steamboats and river disasters. "The peculiarity of the Ohio river [*sic*] which distinguishes it from the Mississippi,

The Ohio River ran from 300 to 600 yards wide. This photograph was taken from the Kentucky side of the river. (Courtesy of the Kentucky Historical Society)

and some others, is its extraordinary gentleness and serenity," Lloyd wrote. He added that "no man who has the least appreciation of natural beauty, ever beheld this river and its diversified shores without a feeling of admiration." The Mississippi River, with nearly two thousand miles of navigable water, also captured the imagination of many, from regular travelers to prominent writers like Mark Twain. As steamboat passenger Edward Jarvis wrote in 1841, "I enjoy this Mississippi. It is grand, it is far more beautiful than I had supposed. There is very little apparent current, but a boiling up of the water . . . It has an appearance of depth . . . quiet, but rolling, and noiseless . . . Like the banks of the lower Ohio, the shores are low . . . the bank is steep, perpendicular, and caving in perpetually."[6]

Although the Mississippi was king, the importance of the Ohio River to nineteenth-century Americans cannot be overstated. In fact, historian Zachary Bennett calls the Ohio "arguably the greatest thoroughfare in the antebellum United States." Furthermore, Bennett believes that for most western residents, "the rhythms of [their] day-to-day existence were tied to that river's

Before the arrival of steamboats, flatboats made the journey down the Ohio and Mississippi Rivers.

ability to facilitate trade and communication." As Anglo settlers populated the Ohio River Valley, inhabitants soon built flatboats to transport goods down the Ohio River to the Mississippi and on to New Orleans. These flatboats, made of logs and guided by a long steering pole, could only travel downstream. Even a youthful Abraham Lincoln helped build a flatboat, and took hogs, wheat, bacon, corn, and other goods down the Mississippi River to sell. Soon, however, those engaging in river commerce constructed keelboats—larger vessels pushed up or downstream by several dozen men with long poles—that could make the journey both ways. On his 1841 voyage, Jarvis remarked that "immense quantities of produce are carried down in these flat-boats. We are now meeting them continually. They are loaded with corn, flour, cattle, oats, pork and horses &c. I should suppose more than half the produce of the upper country is carried down in these boats."[7]

In 1811, steam power reached the Ohio and Mississippi Rivers and completely disrupted transportation. That year, Robert Fulton and Robert Livingston built the steamboat *New Orleans*, which traveled from Pittsburgh to the Crescent City, making it the first steamer to travel on western waters. Leland R. Johnson has called the *New Orleans* the "harbinger of the Industrial Revolution that changed America." That craft's success led to more steamers being constructed along the Ohio River at Pittsburgh, Cincinnati, and Louisville, where thirty-five steamboats were built between 1815 and 1825. Sadly, the *New Orleans* foreshadowed the fate of many river steamboats. In July 1814, it wrecked on a snag—an underwater obstacle—near Baton Rouge, Louisiana. The *New Orleans* was just one of many vessels to sink in this fashion.[8]

Steamboat construction rapidly became an important industry along the Ohio River. The *Comet*, the second steamer to traverse the rivers, reached Louisville in 1813 and went on to New Orleans the following spring. The *Kentucky*, the first steamboat built at Louisville, was constructed in 1815 and measured 112 tons. Louisville manufacturers followed that boat with the *Governor Shelby* two years later. Cincinnati entrepreneurs also entered the business and soon became major players in the steamboat industry. Fifty-two steamers were built there from 1817 to 1827, including the *Vesta* (built in 1817, measuring 203 tons), the *Eagle* (built in 1818 and measuring 118 tons), the *Henderson* (123 tons), and the *Cincinnati* (157 tons). By the 1830s, the steamboat industry was in full swing, and the vessels were ferrying people and goods along both rivers.[9]

In order to maximize profit, steamboat agents and owners packed the vessels with passengers, animals, and freight. "I have been below to see my fellow passengers and find two large flocks of sheep (eighty in each) on the lower ground behind the wheels, a parcel of pigs in boxes one above the other," Edward Jarvis wrote. "I did not see them but heard their infantile grunting, innocent as childhood and as contented, for they but live to eat . . . Also I found six cattle and one calf below and, a little beyond these on the same floor and in the same apartment, some deck passengers. Their bunks were comfortless and cheerless. In one was corn for cattle, in the next a bed for men, and in a third a man by himself; and sometimes in these are women and children." Jarvis also found "fourteen coops of hens" and ducks on board.[10]

Although Ohio River traffic was strong, a natural obstacle hin-

The limestone ledges of the Falls of the Ohio at Louisville impeded river traffic until the Louisville and Portland Canal opened in December 1830. (Courtesy of the Kentucky Historical Society)

dered travel: the Falls of the Ohio. The Falls are limestone ledges of exposed rock that rise in the middle of the river at Louisville. When the river was high, boats with a shallow draft could continue unimpeded; if the water level was low, and the rocks were exposed, vessels had to wait for higher water before continuing on their journey. During times of drought, some boats had to wait at Louisville for weeks until they could cross the Falls. Other boats bold enough to attempt a crossing in times of low water could get snagged on the rocks and stuck. To bypass the Falls, local authorities cut a path around the obstruction. The Louisville and Portland Canal opened in December 1830 when the steamboat *Uncas* passed through. With this success, the *Uncas* proved that unfettered travel to New Orleans was possible. This improvement also led to the expansion of river travel. In 1819, before the canal, twenty-five steamers traversed the Louisville-Cincinnati route. By 1835, more than three hundred steamboats plied the Ohio and Mississippi Rivers. Within five more years, this number jumped

A depiction of the Ohio River at Cincinnati, showing snags in the river, keelboats, and the steamboats *Jamestown, Thomas Jefferson, United States,* and the *General Scott.* (Public Library of Cincinnati and Hamilton County)

to five hundred boats. By the eve of the Civil War, more than seven hundred steamers traveled on western waters.[11]

As the number of boats increased, so too did the growth of towns and villages along the rivers. Steamboats connected these places to larger cities and brought goods, people, and news to those living along the water. The vessels boosted commerce and provided jobs, including ship repair stations, hotels, general stores, saloons, as well as wood yards and coal mines to provide fuel for the boats. The artist John James Audubon, who lived in the Ohio River town of Henderson, Kentucky, for a time, wrote, "This grand portion of our Union is covered with villages, farms, and towns, and steamboats are gliding to and fro over the whole length of the majestic river, forcing commerce to take root and prosper at every spot." It was evident that improved transportation and related infrastructure along the rivers provided positive economic development for the region.[12]

Steamboats like the *Ohio Belle* played an important role in developing commerce, moving people westward, and expanding the United States. Historian Adam I. Kane calls the steamboat "the principal tool used to settle and develop the trans-Appalachian West." This ease of travel led to population growth. In 1810, four states along the Ohio River—Kentucky, Ohio, Indiana, and Illinois—had a population of about 675,000 people. By 1830, as the number of steamboats expanded, the population of these states jumped to more than two million. From 1820 to 1850, Cincinnati grew from 9,600 people to 115,000. In Louisville during the same thirty-year period, the number of residents climbed from four thousand to forty-three thousand. By 1860, Louisville had nearly seventy thousand inhabitants. Steamboats were instrumental in expanding the region's population.[13]

Improved transportation also increased manufacturing and trade along the rivers. Although this affected larger cities like Louisville and Cincinnati, smaller locales also benefitted as trade increased. During one month in 1831, for example, at least 155 steamboats landed at Maysville, an Ohio River town of approximately two thousand residents. One writer in the 1840s contended that the trade was reciprocal. "Steam is crowding our eastern cities with western flour and western merchants," he wrote, "and lading the western steamboats with eastern emigrants and eastern merchandise. It has advanced the career of national colonization and national production, at least a century!"[14]

Steamboat production was an important driver of this economic growth. Pittsburgh, Cincinnati, and Louisville were the major steamboat manufacturing centers, with Louisville producing nearly thirty boats a year. By 1855, as the *Ohio Belle* rode the waters from Cincinnati to New Orleans, more than seven hundred steamers operated on the Mississippi and Ohio Rivers and their tributaries. In 1856 alone, when the disheveled J. B. Jones boarded the *Belle*, more than three thousand steamboats arrived at St. Louis. Also that year there were 288 arrivals and 249 departures along the Cincinnati to New Orleans route, including the *Belle*. In fact, the nation's first "packet line"—a steamboat company transporting people and goods from one set destination to another on a regular schedule—traveled between Cincinnati and

Samuel Clemens, the author known as "Mark Twain," knew firsthand the dangers of steamboat travel. In addition to serving as a steamboat pilot, Clemens's brother died when the steamboat *Pennsylvania* exploded.

Louisville, creating a system that carried people and freight at consistent times. Packet lines added efficiency to riverine transportation, and the *Ohio Belle* was part of an extensive packet line between Cincinnati and New Orleans.[15]

This type of travel, however, was not without risk. First, steamboats could run into snags—logs, rocks, sunken boats, or other underwater obstacles—and sink. Since most nineteenth-century Americans did not know how to swim, a sinking ship was a terrifying and dangerous situation. Moreover, with each boat having massive furnaces and boilers on board to create steam for travel, the risk of fire or explosion was ever present. Boilers were not always well built, and inconsistent metal strength, varying degrees of proper fabrication, and little regulation overseeing construction or safety standards led to horrific accidents. As historian Laura J. Davis explains, "On average, 21 percent of all antebellum riverboats burned or exploded. Between 1847 and 1857 alone, 232 steamers caught fire and another 56 exploded. Between 1816 and 1848, 1,433 people lost their lives to steamboat explosions along western waters." On the Ohio River from 1816 to 1848, including times when various iterations of the *Ohio Belle* steamed up and down the river, forty-five steamboat explosions resulted in 511 deaths. This statistic, however, does not include deaths caused by fires or from boats sinking. In 1856, the year that Jones boarded the *Belle*, the *St. Louis Democrat* estimated that during the first six months of the year there was an average of eight boats lost per month on the Mississippi River. Mark Twain, the scribe of those waters, knew the dangers as both a riverboat pilot and for having lost a family member. His brother, Henry Clemens, died when the steamer he was riding on, the *Pennsylvania*, exploded.[16]

In fact, the nation's worst maritime disaster was caused by an explosion. On April 27, 1865, nearly twelve hundred passengers—most of whom were former Union prisoners of war returning home at the end of the Civil War—died when three boilers on board the *Sultana* burst near Memphis, Tennessee. Scores were killed and scalded in the explosion, and fire spread quickly throughout the boat. W. D. Snow, a US senator from Arkansas who was on board said, "The whole time before the boat was an entire sheet of flame could not have exceeded twenty minutes." The vessel, which was little more than two years old, had been overloaded with passengers. Like the *Ohio Belle*, the *Sultana* had also been constructed in Cincinnati.[17]

Author Charles Dickens described the potential dangers of western American steamboat travel in his *American Notes*. With his English sensibility, Dickens steeled his jaw and embarked on this New World mode of transport. He wrote that

The nation's worst maritime disaster occurred on April 27, 1865, when the steamboat *Sultana* exploded and killed nearly twelve hundred people.

> these western vessels are still more foreign to all the ideas we are accustomed to entertain of boats. I hardly know what to liken them to, or how to describe them . . . the state rooms, jumbled as oddly together as though they formed a small street, built by the varying tastes of a dozen men: the whole is supported on beams and pillars resting on a dirty barge, but a few inches above the water's edge: and in the narrow space between the upper structure and this barge's deck, are the furnace fires and machinery, open at the sides to every wind that blows, and every storm of rain it drives along its path.

Dickens added, "Passing one of these boats at night, and seeing the great body of fire . . . that rages and roars beneath the frail pile of painted wood . . . under the management, too, of reckless men whose acquaintance with its mysteries may have been of six months' standing: one feels directly that the wonder is, not that there should be so many fatal accidents, but that any journey should be safely made." Other famous men, including the Marquis de Lafayette, were also familiar with the dangers of Ohio River steamboats. In May 1825, the French hero and statesman nearly drowned when the steamer he was riding on, the *Mechanic*, hit a snag at night and sank. As the boat went under, Lafayette fell into the Ohio River. Although the marquis was saved, he lost thousands of dollars in currency, as well as his clothing, carriage, and other valuables. But, at least his life was spared.[18]

With these dangers, most steamboats did not last long. Due to rough handling, dangers in the water (snags, debris, ice, sand bars), fire, explosions, and the chance of running into other boats, most only survived for an average of five years. Louis C. Hunter writes that in 1849, 572 steamers traversed western waters. Of these, "only twenty-two were more than five years old." Because of the number of wrecks on the Ohio River, the Canadian journal *Provincial Freeman* called the river "that despicable stream of human misery, woe and destruction . . . A doomed stream it seems to be, as if the avenging angel of the Almighty, had cursed its portentous waters."[19]

In addition to the risks of fire, ice, and explosion, passengers faced additional dangers from machinery and freight. Travelers imbibing too much at the onboard saloon could slip off the boat and disappear into the water. Or, passengers could get caught in the boat's engines. In December 1857, for example, a man named David Lynch traveling on the *North America*, a steamer operating in the northeastern United States, "was caught in the machinery . . . and had his head taken clear off from the body. The body was untouched."[20]

The three boats that traveled under the name *Ohio Belle* from 1839 until 1866 also faced the risk of fire, accident, and explosion and also lost passengers. The first *Belle*, constructed in Cincinnati in 1839, was part of the river traffic that used the Louisville and Portland Canal to haul passengers and freight between Cincinnati and New Orleans. The *Cincinnati Commercial Advertiser and Journal* announced the *Belle* in November 1839, noting that "the 'Ohio Belle' is the name of a splendid new boat, recently built at Cincinnati." In the early 1840s, the *Belle*'s owners were paid seventy-five dollars to deliver mail between the Queen City and New Orleans. Nineteenth-century Americans understood that risk was a regular part of this travel. In the summer of 1841, for example, as the *Belle* left New Orleans, a Cincinnati resident named Wagner fell overboard and drowned. The *Washington Madisonian* simply said, "Such is the daily waste of human life on the Mississippi." Two years later, William Cook, a merchant who shipped goods on the *Belle*, "accidentally stepped off the boat" at two o'clock in the morning and drowned.[21]

Despite the risk of death or dismemberment, passengers from across the nation regularly traveled on the *Ohio Belle*. In 1840, for example, when William Henry Harrison ran against President Martin Van Buren, the Canton, Mississippi, *Whig Advocate* conducted a straw poll on board the *Belle*. With passengers from Virginia, Massachusetts, Kentucky, Indiana, Illinois, Arkansas, Mississippi, Louisiana, Pennsylvania, Maryland, Ohio, Tennessee, New Jersey, Connecticut, Missouri, and New York, the vote stood at 145 for Harrison and 76 for Van Buren. Nine women were also polled, with six supporting Harrison and three for the incumbent Van Buren. The passengers proved to be prescient; Harrison won the election and became the ninth president of the United States. The residences of those taking part in the poll illustrate the breadth of nineteenth-century steamboat travel.[22]

Not all passengers, however, were content. There was at least one suicide on board the first *Ohio Belle*. In April 1842, one traveler wrote that a deck passenger named John Kimmons from Vincennes, Indiana, "deliberately took off his coat, hat, shoes and stockings, while the boat was under way, after dinner, and instead of taking a *siesta*, he jumped over board, swam down stream some two or three hundred yards and sank to rise no more!" Kimmons had recently experienced a bad business trip downriver. He had taken a flatboat full of cargo to New Orleans and faced abysmal sales. He "manifested sights of mental alienation the night before, and gave his pocket book to one of his fellow passengers with a few dollars in it." After giving away his possessions and expressing worry that he would be killed that night or that he might drown himself, fellow Hoosiers on board "laughed at him and thought he was jesting, even when he jumped in."[23]

At the time, Captain Henry A. Jones, who was known as "a gentleman of considerable experience in steamboat navigation,

In February 1840, a newspaper reported that the *Ohio Belle* had "a spacious and commodious cabin." The cabin of the steamboat *James Howard* was equally expansive.

and polite and courteous address," commanded the *Ohio Belle*. Called a "truly fine boat," in February 1840, the *New Orleans Times-Picayune* described the vessel in detail. "Her length of keel is 162 feet; 182 on deck; cabin deck 165; breadth of beam 28; depth of hold 7½; and by custom house measurement is 294 tons," the newspaper wrote. "She has a double engine of 8 feet stroke; five 40 inch boilers, 26 feet in length. Diameter of wheels 26 feet with 11 feet buckets. She has a spacious and commodious cabin, with 44 state rooms, two berths each. Berths in ladies' cabin all double." The reporter added, "There is not so much 'ginger-bread work' about the cabin of the boat as we have seen about others, but we think her all the better for that. For neatness, durability and comfort the Ohio Belle will compare with any thing afloat." The first *Ohio Belle* was luxurious and comfortable, but not gaudy.[24]

Although the fate of the first *Ohio Belle* is unknown, the vessel likely fell victim to a fire or a snag. By late 1843, however, a new steamboat under that name was traveling the Cincinnati to New

Orleans route. The new boat had been constructed in Cincinnati that December for $24,000 (approximately $642,000 today). It was one of thirty-nine steamboats built there that year, with the cost of building all totaling $618,000. Therefore, with each steamboat costing an average of $15,846, the second *Belle* was a higher-end steamboat with luxurious amenities for the passengers.[25]

Throughout the mid-1840s, James Irwin, who had previously commanded the steamboats *Cumberland*, *Ellen Kirkman*, and *Du Quesne*, captained the second *Ohio Belle*. He replaced both Captain Henry A. Jones, who left to command the *Henry Clay*, and Captain William McLain, whom Irwin replaced and who later commanded the *Bostona*. Like most steamboats operating on western waters, in 1844 the *Belle* suffered an accident. Heading up the Mississippi River at night, the *Belle* collided with the schooner *Creole*, which sank with one hundred hogsheads of sugar on board. The *Belle* emerged unscathed. The owners of the *Creole* and their insurance company later sued the *Belle* for the mishap, but the courts placed blame for the accident on the pilot of the schooner who ran his boat into the *Belle*.[26]

The *Belle* received some bad press from that accident and from another incident in which a con man named Taylor slipped away on the boat after stealing $2,500 from a business in Cairo, Illinois. These incidents, however, were quickly forgotten when the *Belle* made national headlines as part of an important 1845 fugitive slave case involving several abolitionist politicians of note.[27]

2

On the Other Side of the World

When the French political scientist Alexis de Tocqueville visited North America, he traveled the Ohio River. "On the right bank of the Ohio," he wrote, "everything is activity, industry; labor is honored; there are no slaves. Cross to the left bank [Virginia or Kentucky] and the scene changes so suddenly that you think yourself on the other side of the world; the enterprising spirit is gone. There, work is not only painful; it's shameful, and you degrade yourself in submitting to it." Like Tocqueville, passengers who traveled on western steamboats for the first time were likely shocked to see how the Ohio River was the region's great dividing line between slavery and freedom. The states north of the river—Ohio, Indiana, and Illinois—were free states, while those to the south—Kentucky and Virginia (including what is now West Virginia) were slave states. Although this difference created political, legal, and philosophical divides, steamboats like the *Ohio Belle* demonstrated the fluidity of that border.[1]

Tocqueville's recognition that the northern side of the river was busier than the southern side is reflected in population statistics. In 1860, Cincinnati had a population of 161,000 and was the seventh-largest city in the United States. The three counties across the Ohio River in the slave state of Kentucky—Boone, Campbell, and Kenton—had smaller populations. Although these counties did not contain the large number of slaves and slave owners found in the Bluegrass region of central Kentucky, the numbers were not

Steamboats, including the *Brooklyn*, docked at Cincinnati. (Public Library of Cincinnati and Hamilton County)

insignificant. In Boone County, with a population of 11,196 residents, 1,745 were slaves and 450 were slave owners (3.88 slaves per owner). This number represented the largest number of enslaved people and owners in the region. Campbell County, with 20,909 residents, had 118 slaves and 49 owners (2.41 slaves per owner). Finally, in Kenton County, which had a population of 25,467, at least 214 owners held 567 enslaved African Americans (2.65 slaves per owner). Therefore, Cincinnati residents were acquainted with Kentucky slaves, especially with those who crossed the Ohio River to find freedom.[2]

Slaves who slipped across the water, however, were not necessarily welcomed by open-armed abolitionists. Although the river provided a legal separation between slavery and freedom, historian Christopher Phillips writes, "Rather than the Ohio River forming an absolute barrier that slavery could not penetrate . . . slavery and white supremacy were interwoven into the fabric of the entire western region. Outright slavery existed in Kentucky and later Missouri, but legislative 'Black Codes' in Illinois, Indiana, and Ohio and support for the legalization of slavery there sharply proscribed African Americans' freedoms and discouraged their residence." Although reaching Ohio soil meant better conditions for Kentucky slaves, life for African Americans living north of the river was difficult. As Matthew Salafia explains, "White Indianans and Ohioans put their racism on display because it served a specific social and political function along the border. White residents of the borderland learned that the border between slavery and freedom was nearly impossible to police, whereas racial boundaries were easier to enforce." Although escaped slaves might find freedom north of the river, Salafia writes, "the link between race and status followed African Americans across the Ohio River border." In many instances, however, there was no chance for runaway slaves to find freedom, for legal cases supporting the enforcement of fugitive slave laws returned them to bondage. The *Ohio Belle* was once involved in such a case.[3]

On January 21, 1845, an enslaved man named Samuel Watson arrived at the Queen City on the *Ohio Belle*. Watson was under the guard of Henry Hoppess, a white Virginian who was transporting Watson from Arkansas to the Old Dominion. Hoppess left the boat, which was tied to the landing at the low water mark on Ohio soil, and went into the city. On his return, he discovered that Watson was missing. Hoppess later found the enslaved man standing at the landing, leaning against a lamppost. Although Watson displayed no intention of trying to escape, seeing the slave standing on northern soil panicked Hoppess, who had hoped to transfer Watson from the *Ohio Belle* to another boat without allowing the slave to touch free land. With Watson on the ground in Cincinnati, the Virginian realized that the slave could potentially slip away, be found by local abolitionists, or could gain his liberty by simply being on free soil. Therefore, to prevent the slave's escape, Hoppess confined Watson in a local jail. The next day, Hoppess took Watson before a magistrate to have him declared a fugitive slave. This status would allow Hoppess to legally reclaim the man before continuing on their journey. Local abolitionists, however, on learning that a slave was confined in Cincinnati, asked a judge to issue a writ of habeas corpus. This action gave Watson a legal

Attorney William Birney was among those who represented fugitive slave Samuel Watson. During the Civil War, Birney served as a Union general.

hearing to determine his standing as an enslaved or free man. If a judge declared Watson to be a slave, he would then appear before a magistrate who would determine his status as a fugitive. With the writ issued, one reporter wrote, Hoppess had to "show cause for the detention of Watson." Hoppess also had to prove that Watson was, indeed, a fugitive slave.[4]

Local abolitionists marshaled their resources and found an outstanding legal team for the enslaved man. The attorneys included the Alabama-born William Birney, whose father, James G. Birney, was an influential Bluegrass State emancipationist. William's father had served in the Kentucky legislature, was a former slave owner, and was a founder of the Kentucky Anti-Slave Society. He was also the founder and editor of the *Philanthropist*, an antislavery newspaper. James Birney eventually moved from

Attorney Salmon P. Chase helped defend fugitive slaves in Cincinnati, including Samuel Watson. Chase became President Abraham Lincoln's secretary of the treasury.

Kentucky to Cincinnati. In 1840, he ran for president as the Liberty Party candidate. His son, William, was a prominent attorney in Cincinnati. During the Civil War, William became a Union general and raised black troops for the Federal cause.[5]

Rounding out the enslaved man's legal team was Salmon P. Chase. A New Hampshire native, Cincinnati attorney, and an active member of the Liberty Party, Chase frequently provided legal support for fugitive slaves. He also had an amazing career after the Hoppess-Watson case. Chase became governor of Ohio in 1855, unsuccessfully ran for the Republican nomination for US president in 1860, and became Abraham Lincoln's secretary of the treasury. In 1864, he became chief justice of the US Supreme Court, a position he held until 1873. Hoppess also had a solid group of attorneys representing him, including Nathaniel McLean, whose father was a congressman and US Supreme Court justice. Like his counterpart William Birney, Nathaniel McLean also became a Union general during the Civil War.[6]

Those attending Watson's hearing remembered Chase's performance. "Mr. S. P. Chase spoke upwards of two hours for Watson," one wrote, "with great ability, clearness and eloquence." Hoppess's legal team argued that Watson was a fugitive slave and that he should be returned to the Virginian under the Fugitive Slave Law. Conversely, Chase and Birney contended that once the slave set foot on Ohio soil, Watson was a free man and never should have been jailed in the first place. Moreover, since the *Belle* was tied to the Ohio shore, Watson's attorneys argued, Watson was not a fugitive because he had traveled from one part of Ohio (the *Belle* on the Ohio shore) to another (the landing by the river). Fugitive slaves, they said, were only those who escaped from a slave state to a free state. Since Watson could not technically escape from one part of Ohio to another, he was not a fugitive slave. Watson's team also posited that the Fugitive Slave Act was unconstitutional because it allowed for "seizure without warrant, trial without jury" and did not let slaves cross-examine witnesses. As reporters heard the intricacies of the case, they determined that Hoppess was "an irresponsible master" for letting Watson onto the shore. As historian Zachary Bennett writes, "Slave traders acknowledged the Ohio's peculiar location by chaining their human cargo on deck; upon reaching the lower Mississippi the enslaved were unfettered and allowed to exercise since slave states surrounded their vessel on all sides." Therefore, Hoppess, who had allowed Watson to wander onto the Ohio shore, was, to many, a negligent enslaver.[7]

Despite the defense team's arguments, the judge sided with Hoppess. He determined that Watson was a fugitive slave. He then remanded Watson back to the Virginian's custody, and sent the case to the magistrate for a fugitive slave case hearing. The decision angered the crowd in the courtroom. "Mr. Hoppess then seized Mr. Watson by the collar and was taking him out," a reporter wrote, "when Mr. Rand, the constable, refused to open the door and let him out, inasmuch as the case had yet to be decided upon by the magistrate." Shortly thereafter, however, Hoppess took Watson before the magistrate. This "produced a great uproar" and "the volunteer constables opened a way through the crowd to another door, and conducted Watson, who was still in the clutches of Hoppess, to the office of the magistrate." The magistrate heard the case, and, under the precepts of the Fugitive Slave Act, allowed Hoppess to take Watson "to Kentucky, beyond the reach of anti-slavery sympathy." When it appeared that the case was lost, Watson asked his attorney William Birney, "Have you done every thing—can nothing more be done?" Birney replied, "Nothing more." Watson then said to Birney, "God Almighty bless you, then, Mr. Birney! I'll never forget you!" He shook Birney's hand. He was then returned to Hoppess, who transported Watson across the Ohio River to Kentucky. There, he locked Watson in the Covington jail for safekeeping and the trip back to enslavement.[8]

The Hoppess-Watson case provided another legal bulwark for the Fugitive Slave Act by determining that if a slave was on a boat tied to free soil, that slave was still considered to be a fugitive. Despite the loss, a group of African Americans from Baker Street Church in Cincinnati gave Salmon Chase a silver pitcher for fighting on Watson's behalf. The pitcher was called "one of the most beautifully designed and magnificent silver pitchers . . . of antique model, with slight chasing of the borders and handle." It was inscribed, "For his various public services in behalf of the oppressed, and particularly for his eloquent advocacy of the rights of Man, in the case of Samuel Watson, who was claimed as a fugitive slave, February 12, 1845."[9]

The crew of the *Ohio Belle*, which had made national headlines as the transport vessel in the Watson case, likely followed the trial with interest. Despite the steamboat's role, business pursuits called. Therefore, the *Belle*, called a "splendid passenger steamer," returned to the rivers, delivering people, goods, mail, and newspapers between Cincinnati and New Orleans. The *Ohio Belle*'s involvement in the Watson case, however, demonstrates another facet of the complexity of the border. As a northern-owned vessel that carried enslaved human cargo, the steamboat's owners profited from, and, therefore, supported, the institution of slavery. In doing so, the *Belle* risked political consequences along this fluid border, which included becoming tied up in fugitive slave cases, like the Watson-Hoppess episode.[10]

The owners of the *Ohio Belle* likely gave little thought to these complexities; yet, as they continued their work, they played a small part in an international conflict. In 1845, the year of the Watson trial, the United States annexed Texas, which Mexico claimed. The United States deployed troops to Texas, and war with Mexico erupted, which lasted until 1848 and cost thousands of lives. The *Belle*, again under the command of Captain Henry A. Jones, transported troops bound for Mexico to New Orleans. In November 1847, the vessel took a company of Ohio volunteers southward. Three months later, the boat earned $1,700 to haul soldiers, "servants" (likely slaves), baggage, and food from barracks on the Ohio River at Newport, Kentucky, to New Orleans. On another run, the *Belle* transported 373 recruits from the Newport Barracks southward, bound for Vera Cruz and Mexico City. In one instance, the vessel let the troops disembark at Louisville as the crew waited to go over the Falls of the Ohio. The soldiers marched through the city to Portland, where they met the *Belle* on the other side of the Falls. "They appeared to be a fine looking body of men," the *Louisville Morning Courier* reported.[11]

In addition to transporting soldiers, the *Belle* continued to haul freight. When the boat delivered items to a city, merchants frequently ran newspaper advertisements promoting what was to be offloaded and sold. One such advertisement in the *New Orleans Daily Crescent* said that one hundred boxes of starch from the *Belle* would be available at a business on Tchoupitoulas Street, a thoroughfare located close to the Mississippi River.[12]

The press that the *Ohio Belle* received in the 1840s, including sales news, the Hoppess-Watson case, and the transportation of soldiers, gave the vessel some renown. By the early 1850s, the *Belle* was famous enough that an accounting teacher used the boat as an example for how to create business ledgers. The teacher outlined the costs of furniture sales from the *Belle*, including three mahogany sofas, two "Tete-a-Tetes," a rocking chair, four arm chairs, two dozen other chairs, fourteen cherry washstands, and

This section of an 1848 panoramic image of Cincinnati shows the second *Ohio Belle*. It was likely destroyed by fire in 1854. (Public Library of Cincinnati and Hamilton County)

fourteen mirrors. No amount of fame, however, could stave off disaster. At some point, likely in 1854, the second *Ohio Belle* was destroyed, probably by fire. A replacement, the third to bear that name, was then constructed. It was this boat that the intoxicated Mississippian J. B. Jones boarded in 1856.[13]

3

And the Mother Rejoiced

When shipbuilders constructed the third and final *Ohio Belle*, a 406-ton, side-wheeled steamer, in Cincinnati in 1855, the Queen City was booming. Settled in 1788, the city's population had ballooned to more than 160,000 people within seventy years. This included many German immigrants, who by 1860 comprised about one-third of the city's residents. Steamboats began making regular trips to and from Cincinnati in 1818, and this expansion of river traffic and increased trade was a primary driver of this population growth. The influx of more people also led to what historian Erica Hannickel calls "a remarkable cultural flowering" of the arts and "cultural clubs" in Cincinnati. In 1831, however, as the Queen City's growth began in earnest, Alexis de Tocqueville wrote, "All that there is of good or bad in American society is to be found there." Despite the blossoming of the arts, it was also a rough and bustling western river town.[1]

A wide array of businesses thrived in Cincinnati, with many of them fueled by steamboat traffic. In the 1840s, as the second *Ohio Belle* transported goods up and down the river, advertisements in *Kimball and James' Business Directory* listed the variety of local traders and manufacturers. Auctioneers, banks, booksellers, boot sellers, soap makers, real estate agents, brush and bellow manufacturers, publishing companies, chair and cabinet makers, cider and vinegar dealers, china and glass salesmen, coal and brick merchants, grain and food wholesalers, confectioners, rope makers, "daguerreotype miniature takers," dentists, druggists, dye houses, wineries, engravers, brass foundries, and dozens of

French political scientist Alexis de Tocqueville said of Cincinnati, "All that there is of good or bad in American society is to be found there."

other businesses produced goods for an expanding United States. Despite all of these ventures, however, pork was king in the Queen City. In the early 1840s about a quarter million hogs were slaughtered there annually, with the processed pork exported across the country. The growing economy led to innovations and infrastructure, including gaslights for homes in 1842 and lighted streets two years later that illuminated Main Street "from the river to the canal." That same decade, lead water pipes replaced the old log ones. Businesses continued to flourish, and in 1847, more than four thousand steamboats docked there. Shortly thereafter, historian Louis C. Hunter writes, "Cincinnati had become the main division point and principal center of steamboat operations on the Ohio River." *Lloyd's Steamboat Directory* soon proclaimed that Cincinnati was "the largest city on the western waters" and that "it has become the principal gathering and distributing point in the valley of this great river." The *Belle* played a part in this growth.[2]

As *Lloyd's* relates, when the third *Ohio Belle* was built, no western city along the Ohio River surpassed Cincinnati. The town ran for four miles along the water and included an impressive wharf for the thousands of steamboats that visited annually. "At the foot of Main Street is the public landing for steamboats"; *Lloyd's* wrote, "it is an open area of ten or twelve acres, with twelve hundred feet front. The wharf is paved with stone from low water mark to the sidewalk, affording a dry and substantial landing to the large fleet of boats plying to and from this great metropolis." Manufacturing continued to fuel Cincinnati's economy, with local products being valued at about $71 million. Pork production also remained strong. In 1855, when the *Belle* was constructed, 460,000 hogs were slaughtered there, producing tens of thousands of barrels of pork and bacon. Steamboat production was also critical to the city's success. Manufacturers built nearly three hundred boats in Cincinnati during the 1840s and 288 in the 1850s, including the third *Ohio Belle*.[3]

When the new *Belle* hit the rivers, the steamboat was lauded for its luxury. The *New Orleans Daily Crescent* called it a "fine regular passenger steamer," and "comfortable and commodious." The *Evansville Daily Journal* was equally impressed, praising the vessel as an "elegant passenger packet." Like her predecessors, the steamer was based in Cincinnati and ran to New Orleans and back, with stops in Louisville, Cairo, and other towns. Arrangements to travel or ship goods on the *Belle* could be made in Cincinnati or in New Orleans via John E. Hyde and Co., located near the Mississippi River at 66 Poydras Street. The boat's arrivals and departures were also printed in newspapers along the route. There was quite a bit of competition along that run, with multiple vessels making the trek between the Queen City and the Big Easy. These included the *Nick Thomas*, *Europa*, *Madison*, *William Noble*, *Antelope*, *Golden Gate*, *Statesman*, *Queen of the West*, and dozens more.[4]

It cost the owners of the *Belle* about $200 a day to run the ship. The *Belle* could travel from Cincinnati to New Orleans in about twenty days, faster if the river was high and the current strong. If the water level was too low, the ship would wait in port towns for the river to rise before traveling on. The boat delivered wine, sugar, stoves, Osage orange seeds, furniture, whiskey, food, and a myriad of other goods. If the *Belle* carried a good load, local papers reported the news. In March 1855, for example, the *Belle* passed Evansville, Indiana, on the way to New Orleans "with a full trip of freight." In another instance, the ship made headlines when it transported the first "steam fire-engine" from Cincinnati to New Orleans, which the *Daily Crescent* called a "much-talked-of revolutionary apparatus." With the threat of fire ever present, residents were pleased that it was "at last in town." It cost the city of New Orleans $250 in freight charges to procure the engine. Although a boat's full load made news, word also spread when freight was lacking. For many, these reports served as a barometer for the overall health of river commerce. In December 1855, for example, the *Belle* stopped in Evansville. "The Ohio Belle was here Saturday morning, for Cincinnati with a good load on board for New Orleans," it was reported. "She had room, however, for a good deal of pork, &c. from this place." City leaders and merchants always hoped that steamboats left their shores at full capacity, taking their town's goods elsewhere to sell.[5]

In addition to freight, the *Belle* carried dozens of passengers each trip, including merchants, tourists, and travelers. Passengers sometimes included schemers hoping to make money. George Devol, a noted Mississippi River gambler, once took the *Belle* out of New Orleans. Devol determined that the boat "was full of good looking suckers." He started playing the card game Monte in the cabin. Passengers bet on the game, but so did the captain, which troubled the gambler. Devol said to him, "You are the captain of the boat, and I do not want to bet with you." Devol feared that if the captain lost, he would shut down the game. The captain insisted and bet $500. "I told him not to bet if the loss would distress him," Devol wrote, "when he told me it was his money. I told him to turn the card, for I saw it was the only way to get rid of him. He turned, and lost; then he got mad, and made me close up."[6]

With his game halted, Devol went out of the cabin, found the captain, and told him that he would return his money. The relieved captain was shocked at the gambler's generosity and allowed Devol to play again. The gambler asked the captain to win his money back, so the captain returned to the cabin, bet on a game, and won. This encouraged more bettors, including one "sucker" passenger who bet $1,500. Devol wrote that the player "was so nervous that he turned the wrong card. It made him so sick that he went out on the guards and threw up his supper. The balance of the suckers did not want to get sick, so I closed up; but if it had not been for the Captain's first play, I would have done a much better business on that boat."[7]

That captain was John Sebastian, who was master and part owner of the *Belle*. Born in Louisville on September 27, 1817, Sebastian was the grandson of a Virginia-born minister who moved to Kentucky when it was still part of the Old Dominion. His father, also named John, was born in Louisville in 1791, and his mother, Catherine Hinkle, was also a Kentuckian. Sebastian grew up with few educational opportunities but was self-motivated. His obituary later stated that his "strong natural powers . . . led him to a useful and successful career." At age fifteen, Sebastian went to work on the Ohio River, learning how to pilot a steamboat. It became a family affair; two of his brothers, George and Charles, also became steamboat pilots. In 1844 John married Emily Hinkle—who was likely a distant cousin—and their union was blessed with six daughters and two sons. Within six years, Sebastian and his family were living across the river from Cincinnati in Newport, Kentucky. He was making a good living as a steamboat pilot and owned $5,000 in real estate. Sebastian eventually moved to the Queen City, where he remained until after the Civil War.[8]

In March 1856, when Sebastian's crew guided the *Ohio Belle* to Smithland and picked up the Mississippian J. B. Jones, the weather was cold and the river icy. It had been a bitter winter. Several weeks earlier, the temperature had dropped to twenty-one degrees below zero. The icy river and the news of a recent steamboat accident along their path made for a tense journey. Just a few days earlier, the *Henry Lewis* made national headlines when it collided with another boat and sank in the Ohio River. Because the *Henry Lewis* also plied the Cincinnati to New Orleans route, the passengers and crew probably paid close attention to the story. The news of the *Henry Lewis* was made even more memorable because of a horrific event tied to the disaster: the fate of the escaped slave Margaret Garner, on board the *Henry Lewis*, who had previously murdered her daughter to keep the girl out of slavery.[9]

The collision of the *Henry Lewis* and the *E. Howard* was called "one of the most wild and terrific ever experienced on the western waters." On March 8, 1856, the *Lewis*, heading for New Orleans from Cincinnati, reached a bend in the river at Troy, Indiana, a small town of about three hundred inhabitants located thirty miles east of Owensboro, Kentucky. The three-year-old *Henry Lewis* was called a "first class New Orleans steamer." Forty passengers and twenty-four crew members were on board, and the boat was laden with "several hundred tons of pork, with large quantities of oil, lard, cheese, and such other produce as is usually shipped from Cincinnati." The goods were piled so high on the deck that the cabin was nearly obscured. Also on the vessel were four enslaved African Americans, accompanied by a US marshal who was to prevent their escape.[10]

The slaves on the *Henry Lewis* had previously made national headlines as part of a shocking fugitive slave case. Because of that episode, their master, Archibald Gaines of Boone County, Kentucky, was sending the enslaved Margaret Garner, her infant daughter, and two other members of her family to a plantation in Arkansas. In January 1856, two months before being forced on the *Henry Lewis*, the slaves had crossed the frozen Ohio River—the "ice bridge" that took fifty-three days to crack—from Kentucky to Ohio in order to escape slavery.[11] Margaret Garner, who was pregnant, braved the ice with her four children, her husband, and her in-laws. They escaped to Ohio, but when federal marshals closed in on their hiding place in Cincinnati, Garner cut the throat of her two-year-old daughter to keep the girl out of slavery. The marshals apprehended Garner before she could kill the other children.

Garner's ensuing trial as a fugitive slave made national headlines and shone additional light on the brutality of slavery. During the trial, abolitionist Levi Coffin noted that Garner held a baby. "The babe she held in her arms was a little girl, about nine months old," he wrote. "The babe was continually fondling [Garner's]

The enslaved Margaret Garner, who escaped from Kentucky to Ohio, killed her daughter to keep the girl out of slavery. Garner lost another child—whom she may have drowned—when the steamboat *Henry Lewis* sank on the Ohio River.

face with its little hands, but she rarely noticed it, and her general expression was one of extreme sadness." After the hearing, Garner, with the baby still in her arms, was returned to enslavement. Authorities in Ohio, however, including Governor Salmon P. Chase—who had helped defend the fugitive slave Henry Watson when he wandered off the *Ohio Belle*—wanted to charge Garner with murder. Instead, her owner sent Margaret and her family to Arkansas on the *Henry Lewis*. On being returned to bondage, Coffin wrote, Garner "could see nothing but woe for herself and her children."[12]

At 4:00 a.m. on March 8, the *Henry Lewis* moved into the bend at Troy, Indiana. As the boat rounded the turn, it collided with the *E. Howard*, a four-year-old Nashville packet boat that was traveling upstream carrying sugar. The *Howard* either had bad luck or bad pilots; the vessel had previously sunk two other boats and had also been sunk twice. In striking the *Henry Lewis*, the pilot of the *Howard* contended that he could not see the *Lewis*'s lights because the decks of that boat were piled high with freight.[13]

The sleeping passengers on the *Henry Lewis*, including Margaret Garner, her family, and the US marshal, were violently awakened when the *Howard* hammered into their vessel. One reporter wrote that they "hurried forth amid the crashing of timbers, the hissing of steam, the hurry to and fro, the alarm of fires and cries of drowning wretches, to find themselves surrounded by death in its most hideous forms."[14]

The *Lewis* spun in the water. The impact jostled the mountainous pile of freight wedged on the deck, which fell on the roof of the cabin and crushed it, injuring many passengers with broken glass and debris. Three thousand dollars' worth of chickens, stacked high upon one another in coops on the deck, was all lost. The cabin split in half, the boat caught fire, and as the rolling freight shifted, the steamer tipped partially over. Within three minutes, the *Lewis* sank in twenty-three feet of water, leaving only the top hurricane deck protruding above the current. Passengers scrambled to reach that high point as the vessel came to a rest on the bottom of the river, seventy-five yards from the shore.[15]

As passengers fell into the freezing water, some of the crew jumped into action. John McGeary, a cook on the *Lewis*, saved one female passenger and his own brother, who also worked on the boat. The crew of the *E. Howard* pulled people out of the river as well.[16]

Margaret Garner's infant, a child named Cilla, was not so fortunate. After the *Howard* struck the boat, Garner and her family were unshackled to save them from drowning within the bowels of the ship. Garner reached the deck and fell into the river. Although she was saved, her baby was lost. A reporter, who noted that Garner had previously murdered one of her other children, wrote that "the child was drowned and the others [slaves] saved. The mother, it is stated, exhibited no other feeling than joy at the loss of her child." It was also reported that Garner, to keep this child from slavery, threw the infant overboard. "God took it," a newspaper wrote, "and the mother rejoiced."[17]

It was estimated that thirty-five of the forty passengers were saved. Ten to twelve of the crew drowned. The US marshal who guarded Garner was spared because other passengers chopped a hole in the roof of his cabin and pulled him to safety. In fact, the marshal had an unlikely savior. Before the accident, the marshal, a man named Butts from Covington, Kentucky, swaggered around the boat, showing off "an immense amount of cutlery and fire arms, with which he expressed himself resolved to slaughter whole armies of Abolitionists." At one point, Butts had an intense argument with another passenger about the Garner case. This man evidently led the effort to save the marshal, and when they pulled Butts out of his cabin, the man exclaimed, "Hallo, Butts, is that you? D—n you, if I'd known that, you might have drowned." In addition to showcasing the prevalence of firearms on board steamboats in the 1850s, the episode also demonstrates the tension between those who, when brought together on the border by steam travel, supported the institution of slavery and those who did not.[18]

Shortly after the collision, Margaret Garner and her surviving family members were put on the steamer *Hungarian* and sent to Arkansas. Although Ohio officials tried to extradite Garner for the murder of her daughter, Garner remained enslaved in the south. By 1858, she had been sold to another owner. Later that year she reportedly died of typhoid fever in Mississippi. The tragic story of Garner and her family has inspired artists and writers, including author Toni Morrison, whose novel *Beloved* is based on Margaret Garner's tale. Although Garner's experience illustrates the fluidity of the border and the grim fate of some fugitive slaves, her presence on the *Henry Lewis* also shows how owners like Archibald Gaines used the rapidity of steam travel to protect their chattel property. In addition to helping owners quickly send borderland slaves who were flight risks to the Deep South, it also enabled them to keep enslaved people charged with crimes away from authorities. In both cases—securing a flight risk and eluding authorities—it meant that steamboats played a role in protecting owners' property.[19]

When the *Ohio Belle* neared Troy, Indiana, the passengers

The actress Matilda Heron, famous for her role in
Camille, initially saved J. B. Jones from being lynched
by the crew of the *Ohio Belle*. (Courtesy of the Folger
Shakespeare Library)

surely saw the hurricane deck of the sunken *Henry Lewis* rising
from the icy water. Among those whispering about the enslaved
Margaret Garner—her name was typically unlisted in newspaper
accounts and, therefore, unknown to most—was the actress Matilda Heron, who was on her way to New Orleans to reprise her
famous role. Born on December 1, 1830, in County Londonder-
ry, Ireland, Heron was the daughter of a farmer who moved to
Philadelphia when she was twelve years old. Her father became a
prosperous lumber merchant, which gave Matilda the opportunity to study theater. She honed her craft for several years, made her
acting debut in Philadelphia, and then performed with multiple
traveling theater companies. In 1854, Heron moved to London,

England. During a trip to France, she saw *Camille* performed in Paris. Moved by the play, she translated the work from French to English and published her script. On October 3, 1855, she performed it in Philadelphia to rave reviews. Three months later, she took it to St. Louis. It proved to be the role that defined her as an artist.[20]

Alberta Lewis Humble, who wrote a biographical sketch of Heron, said that the actress was an impassioned, groundbreaking performer. "Matilda Heron's impulsive, quixotic nature aided her in developing a style of acting new for her day," Humble writes. "Breaking with convention, she followed her feelings rather than the rules of elocution. Her emotion-charged acting and personal magnetism, particularly in the role of Camille with which she became so closely identified, hypnotized audiences and critics alike." An earlier biographer called the actress "an erratic genius," while James Fisher and Felicia Hardison Londre contend that "Heron was said to have founded the 'emotional school' of acting." Heron was respected for her work, which through the role of Camille gave her success and fame.[21]

Before Heron boarded the *Ohio Belle*, she maintained a busy schedule, performing in St. Louis on January 7, 1856. After another performance there, a reporter admired the emotional acting that Heron had perfected. He wrote that she appeared "with that subdued simplicity and holy earnestness by which the genius of a noble soul awakens sympathetic feelings, and she swayed St. Louis like a Queen. Her Camille was rendered with such magical affect that the audience, spell bound by her magnetic will, not only mingled their tears with hers, but joined in the hectic cough of the consumption she represented." Heron performed in St. Louis for six weeks, "during the extreme cold weather," and "charmed" her audiences. She then went to Cincinnati's National Theatre, where more good reviews followed. From there, Heron took the *Ohio Belle*, bound for the Crescent City. On March 10, the *Washington Evening Star* reported that "Matilda Heron has gone to New Orleans. Her engagement at Cincinnati was popular and profitable." Another Washington newspaper, the *Sentinel*, also noted the change of venue "after a prolonged engagement of extraordinary success." The reporter added that "Miss Heron is a woman of genius, and has won her way through all impediments to a proud dramatic position." If her jewelry was any indication, her work was also profitable. Two months later, four of her diamond rings were stolen at the St. Charles Hotel in New Orleans.[22]

Heron still had those rings on her fingers when J. B. Jones boarded the *Ohio Belle* at Smithland. When Jones checked his luggage, he told the crew that he was the son of a Mississippi planter. In the slave-owning, honor-bound South, Jones's aristocratic birth immediately gave him cachet on the vessel. Initial reactions to him were favorable. According to one traveler on the *Ohio Belle*, "Jones is an intelligent-looking, handsome young man, apparently about 22 or 23 years of age, says he lives in Marshall County, Mississippi." After dropping off his bags, Jones, who was reputedly drunk when he boarded, went to the onboard saloon and downed more liquor.[23]

At approximately 11:00 a.m., while the *Ohio Belle* was between Smithland and Cairo, Jones stumbled out of the saloon and went to the boat's barber for a shave. To pay, Jones gave the barber a twenty-dollar bill. The barber went to the boat's clerk, Hiram E. Stevens, for change. Stevens examined the money, proclaimed it was a counterfeit bill, and refused to accept it. When the barber told Jones that his money had been rejected, the irritated Mississippian produced a ten-dollar bill. Stevens also returned that money, citing that it, too, was counterfeit.[24]

Like Captain Sebastian, Stevens had spent much time on the river. Therefore, he kept a wary eye out for gamblers, confidence men, and thieves. Before becoming clerk of the *Ohio Belle*, Stevens was captain of the steamboat *Eliza*, another boat that ran passengers and trade to New Orleans. "Eliza" was, seemingly, an unlucky name for a boat; several vessels of that name experienced wrecks and other disasters. In 1842, one *Eliza*—not Stevens's steamer—hit a snag on the Mississippi near the mouth of the Ohio River and sank in two minutes. Dozens perished. Ten years after that, the *Eliza No. 2*, also not Stevens's boat, experienced horror when two brothers, Moses and Robert Kelley, axe-murdered several people onboard. The Kelleys were hanged in Hawesville,

Kentucky, for the crime, and it was later reported that Robert Kelley's skull served as "a paper weight in a local newspaper office" for a time. Two years after the Kelley murders, the *Eliza No. 2* sank after hitting a snag twenty-five miles below Mobile, Alabama, and lost scores of cotton bales. That same year, another *Eliza* ran into the *Kentucky*, a ferryboat at Covington, Kentucky, while heading up the Ohio River on a foggy morning. In January 1855 that boat again hit a snag at Plum Point, Mississippi. Loaded with cargo, the steamboat "sunk up to her hurricane deck." Newspaper reports were unclear as to the number of casualties, but it was feared that many lives were lost. Although it is unknown if Stevens commanded the boat during this final accident, the disaster may explain his move from being master of the *Eliza* to clerk of the *Ohio Belle* in 1856. Although "Eliza" may have been a doomed name for a steamboat, Stevens's luck completely ran out on the *Ohio Belle*.[25]

The cause of Stevens's misfortune was the supposed counterfeit bill. When the barber told Jones that Stevens had rejected the money, the Mississippian demanded to speak to the clerk. One witness later said, "The strange man flew, as it were, into a rage, and rushed out of the shop in a wild and desperate manner." Jones found Stevens and asked the clerk why he thought the bill was counterfeit. Stevens replied that he recognized the bill as a forgery. Jones became more enraged, and cursed and screamed at the clerk. Sebastian wrote that Jones "abused Stevens, using such language and in such a boisterous manner, as to call the attention of the passengers and to annoy all who heard him." A reporter later wrote that Jones "paced the cabin, abusing the boat, and Capt. Stevens particularly, using vile and improper language in hearing of the ladies." Stevens told the Mississippian to calm down or he would remove him from the cabin. Jones, however, kept ranting. Stevens then grabbed Jones's arm, told the southerner that "he had violated the rules of the boat," and walked him out, Sebastian wrote, "forward on the boiler deck."[26]

After Stevens escorted the Mississippian out of the cabin, he told Jones that if he calmed down, they could resolve the issue. Jones, however, was in no mood for a compromise. Instead, he pulled a pistol from his pocket and shot Stevens in the left side of his chest, just below the armpit. The *Cairo Weekly Times* reported that "the ball entered between the fourth and fifth ribs passing through the left lung and in all probability through his heart." With the black powder smoke still swirling around Stevens, Jones turned and ran. The clerk stumbled after Jones for a dozen steps before collapsing. Passengers, roused by the gunshot, found the injured clerk and carried him into a cabin. A doctor on board examined the wound and determined that there was no hope of survival. Captain Sebastian wrote that Stevens "made two or three efforts to speak, and was understood to say that he wished the wound bathed, but he spoke so indistinctly that those present could not understand definitely what he wished to say. He lived some fifteen or twenty minutes." A Cincinnati newspaper wrote that Stevens "was extensively known and beloved and respected in this community."[27]

And now, thanks to the drunken Jones and an argument over counterfeit money, Stevens was dead.

4

Boasting of the Bloody Deed

Jones's pistol shot proved that the luxurious surroundings of a steamboat were not free from violence and murder. Unsurprisingly, the shooting on the *Ohio Belle* was not an isolated incident. Instead, and as a reflection of nineteenth-century society in general, Stevens's death was just one of many deadly acts perpetrated on western waters. Like the general public, crew members and passengers could have a propensity for violence. In addition, the combination of alcohol and concealed weapons on board proved to be a volatile mix. Fights, shootings, stabbings, intentional drownings, clubbings with firewood, and other lethal episodes occurred despite the deluxe accommodations.[1]

Violence had long been perpetrated on western rivers. Cave-in-Rock, a large stone opening located on the banks of the Ohio River in southern Illinois, was a known den for thieves, murderers, and river pirates. Among the worst of these outlaws were the infamous Harpe brothers, who are believed to be among the first serial murderers in the United States. In addition to killing people in Tennessee, Illinois, and Kentucky, the Harpes once holed up at Cave-in-Rock and murdered travelers along the Ohio River.[2]

Violence along the water was later reflected in songs sung by steamboat workers. "Some ole boy in this town," / one stanza went, "I wisht he was dead an' gone, / I'd drug that razor across his throat, / My Baby'd pay my fine, / My Baby'd pay my fine." The narrator of another "roustabout" song relates that ever "since I killed a man," the murderer had been "Skippin' an' dodgin' right through the land, Babe." A third tune notes how the

C. P. Riley, a crew member of the *Ohio Belle*, severely injured steamboat captain Charles Sebastian by bludgeoning him with a bottle. Sebastian was sent to Louisville on the *Jacob Strader* to recover. (Public Library of Cincinnati and Hamilton County)

devil killed "Vinie" over "a Duke cigarette." The devil was sent to the gallows, which he climbed silently at the song's end. "Now you've killed Vinie, an' you got to leave this worl."[3]

Historian Edward Ayers writes that "aggression flourished most democratically where gambling and drinking flourished." Therefore, steamboats were floating crucibles for violence, where the blending of liquor, card games, knives, and pistols sparked hostility. The later actions of C. P. Riley, who served as the second clerk on the *Ohio Belle* when Jones killed Stevens, illustrate how alcohol and a proclivity for violence among some boatmen could be dangerous. On March 23, 1861, five years after Hiram Stevens's death on the *Ohio Belle*, Captain John Sebastian's youngest brother, Charles (also a steamboat captain) went to the Broadway Exchange Hotel in Cincinnati. There he encountered Riley, whose service on the *Ohio Belle* had been interrupted by the Civil War. Riley asked Charles to join him for a drink. Charles sat down, and Riley gave him a pour. "As [Charles] Sebastian was in the act of drinking," a newspaper reported, "Riley raised the bottle and knocked Sebastian down, cutting one of his eyes nearly out. Riley then kicked him and made his escape." Authorities issued a warrant for Riley's arrest. Doctors feared that Charles, who was carted back to his home in Louisville on the steamboat *Jacob Strader* to recover, would lose his eye. The cause of the assault was unknown (perhaps Charles's brother John had insulted Riley on the *Ohio Belle* or fired him), but alcohol consumption surely fueled the attack, just as it did when Jones killed Stevens.[4]

Although Charles Sebastian was terribly injured, the attack did not end his career. Three years later, Charles was captain of the *City Belle*. At some point, however, he lost his captaincy and again became a steamboat pilot. By 1869 he was piloting the *John H. Groesbeck*, a boat that his brother John had commanded at the end of the Civil War. Shortly thereafter, Charles worked on the *Louisiana* and the *Edinburgh*. In late 1872, Charles had his pilot's license suspended for three months for ramming the *Mollie Moore* into a ferryboat. He ignored this suspension, however, and took the *Armadillo* from Cincinnati to New Orleans. Authorities learned of this infraction, and when Charles ignored a summons from riverboat inspectors, the case was handed over to the Cincinnati district attorney. Legal authorities evidently had more pressing matters, and Charles's case was dismissed on his payment of court costs. Charles then returned to the water and piloted the *Henry Probasco* and the *Nick Longworth*. In May 1874, while aboard the *Longworth*, Charles "suddenly [became] ill with inflammation of the bowels" and died in his cabin. He was fifty-four years old and was survived by his wife and four grown children. He was buried at Cave Hill Cemetery in Louisville.[5]

As Riley's assault on Charles Sebastian demonstrates, crew members attacking steamboat captains was not unknown. Many steamboat workers lived a rough, transient life, and some surely sought retribution for an officer's harsh discipline. In July 1866, some crew members "treacherously assaulted" steamboat captain Hugh Davis of the *Mollie Able* at St. Louis. Davis had evidently fired at least one of the men. In the attack, Davis "was severely, but not dangerously injured."[6]

Transporting soldiers on steamboats could also be perilous as armed troops, cooped up and bored, were confined in cramped spaces. In May 1846, for example, as the *Galveston* steamed toward the Mexican War, one soldier attacked another, "cutting him in the abdomen and through the arm and breast." A soldier saw "the poor fellow's bowels instantly protruding. Our surgeon replaced them and sewed him up. Poor fellow, he died at half-past one that night." After the ship's captain performed a brief funeral, the slain soldier was buried at sea. The troops, surprised by the violent outburst, had no idea what provoked the attack.[7]

Hostility among crew members could also lead to homicide. In 1846 an engineer on the *Ohio Mail* bickered with a fireman before striking him with a piece of firewood. This knocked the fireman "against the furnace, and burned him so severely as to cause his death yesterday morning in great agony." The engineer fled the boat when it arrived at Portland, outside of Louisville. Two years later on the *Talleyrand*, a deckhand named Dennis Higgins had an altercation with another man and killed him with "a billet of wood." Higgins was arrested but escaped. He was later recognized by two crew members while working on the *Iroquois*, and was arrested. In 1859, Owen Dennegen stabbed and killed John Moore, a fireman on the *W. A. Violett*. Dennegen slipped off of the boat and escaped. Other perpetrators who tried to evade capture were not so fortunate. In an era when few learned to swim, escaping from a moving steamboat was a dangerous proposition. In 1852, as the *Yuba* traveled from Cincinnati to New Orleans, a passenger "became troublesome." Watchman William Jenkins took the traveler out of the cabin. The passenger promptly pulled a bowie knife and stabbed Jenkins, killing him. The murderer jumped overboard to escape and was "found drowned in the river the day after the murder." Even enslaved men transported on steamboats were not immune to homicide. On the *Magnolia* in 1849, a slave named Henry killed another named Sam. In the ensuing trial, Henry claimed self-defense, and the case was dismissed.[8]

As in the case when C. P. Riley bludgeoned Charles Sebastian, alcohol was frequently a factor when crew members tangled. In 1853, crewman John Gill killed fellow worker John Murphy on the *Isabel*. Murphy was known as "an overbearing, quarrelsome, drunken bully." He had been drinking and threatened Gill before stealing Gill's blanket. He then chased Gill up to the deck with a knife. Murphy then went to his bunk and proclaimed that he would kill Gill the next time he saw him. When Gill went down to the bunks, Murphy moved in to attack. The threatened man struck Murphy in the forehead with a large piece of coal, killing him. Gill was later acquitted by reason of self-defense. In 1853, in another alcohol-laden incident, the steamboat *St. Louis* picked up a flatboat crew to transport them to Cairo, Illinois. The men drank heavily, played cards, and when a fight erupted over the game, Robert Crawford beat Joseph Carter to death.[9]

Steamboat officers also became involved in melees with the crew. In November 1858, the captain of the schooner *Albatross* shot a deckhand in the stomach. Both were drunk, and the deckhand had reputedly been "abusive" to the captain. The officer ordered him off the boat, and when the crewman refused, the captain shot him. When the captain was arrested, he was "still so excited by liquor and passion that he boasted of the bloody deed."[10]

Tales of steamboat violence appeared all too often in newspapers across the country. In late 1853, nine deckhands from the *Louisiana* killed crew member E. Anderson on the *Lake Erie* after Anderson complained that the nine were treating women "improperly." Witnesses "saw Anderson robbed and thrown overboard." The nine men, however, were acquitted due to a lack of evidence. Two years later, two workers on the *W. N. Sherman* stabbed and killed a nineteen-year-old crew member after an argument. Four months after that, a member of the *Belle Sheridan* was beaten to death with a stick of firewood while on board the *Gem* docked at New Orleans. The assailant dropped the wood by the body and "coolly walked ashore." Murders and disappearances became so worrisome that by mid-1856, the *Pittsburgh Dispatch* contended that an investigation "would lead to the disclosure of the fact that not a few of the deck hands found drowned in the river, are murdered on steamboats." The newspaper added that "we have personally witnessed several instances of outrageous brutality and oppression towards deck hands and laborers, by steamboat mates."[11]

Southern honor culture influenced violence on steamboats, at least among members of the Dixie-born "bowie knife and pistol gentry." This culture also played a role in Jones's murder of Stevens and influenced how some southerners reacted to the killing. Honor was indelibly bound to one's reputation. Therefore, any behavior that insulted a southerner and bruised his honor could cause a hair-triggered, violent reaction. This was especially true if the insulted man was of a higher social standing than the person who slighted him. In February 1856, for example, the *New York Daily Tribune* reported that "a notorious fellow named Johnson Lyman, alias Lyme, from New-York, was shot on board a river steamboat by a Texan named Craig, whom he had insulted." This culture of honor, insult, and retribution was the flame that lit the fuse surrounding Stevens's murder.[12]

As the shooting of Lyman indicates, insults and other behavior that impugned a southerner's honor could lead to a quick and violent response. Although honor killings are often seen to be a distinctively southern phenomenon, the concept of honor and its application was not confined to that region or to a particular class. Historian Lorien Foote, for example, explains that northerners had their own version of honor culture, regardless of social standing, that led to violent exchanges. Foote writes that "few northern men dueled, but they would fight and kill for honor." Moreover, as historian Joanne B. Freeman notes, during the early nineteenth century, "Northerners were as well versed in this [honor] code as southerners; it was in their utilization of violence that they differed most noticeably." However, as Richard F. Hamm explains, "Honor had once been present all across the nation, but by the middle of the nineteenth century, it was increasingly being seen as a distinctive aspect of southern society." Honor-related violence was also overwhelmingly male. Therefore, in addition to this study that examines honor as "a distinctive aspect of southern society," it is also focused on male-oriented violence.[13]

When news that Jones had killed Stevens spread, the idea of a Mississippian perpetrating violence on board a steamboat would not have surprised many antebellum Americans. While visiting Mississippi in 1861, William Russell said that he was "indeed in the land of Lynch-law and bowie-knives, where the passions of men have not yet been subordinated to the influence of the tribunals of justice." Mississippians engaging in violence was also widely reported out of state, which included an 1838 incident in Kentucky where three Mississippians were tried for the murder of a Louisville tailor and another man. The Mississippians, including a prominent judge, had argued with the tailor over the fit of a wedding suit. This altercation later led to murder in the barroom of the Galt House Hotel in Louisville. Whether this coverage of Mississippi violence was fair or not, many believed that members of the Magnolia State planter class, like Jones, had the personalities described by one Alabama newspaper editor. For this newspaperman, they were part of the "testy touch-wood gentry, who are ready to draw a pistol if a cat should tread on their toe."[14]

In 1856, the year that Jones killed Stevens, Americans had a clear understanding about southerners' touchiness and violence caused by infractions of honor. That May, in an incident that shocked the nation, South Carolina congressman Preston Brooks caned Massachusetts senator Charles Sumner in the US Senate chamber. Brooks beat Sumner because of comments the northern senator had made about Brooks's relative, Senator Andrew Butler, during a speech about admitting Kansas as a free or slave state. Taking up the banner of honor for his insulted kinsman (and for his region, since the expansion of slavery was on the line), Brooks savagely pummeled Sumner until the Massachusetts senator collapsed unconscious, grievously injured. Brooks's cane was shattered in the assault, and well-wishers from across the South sent the congressman dozens of new canes, including one inscribed, "Hit Him Again." Thanks to Brooks, in 1856, Americans fully understood that honor could spark violence. Not only did this brutality play out in the halls of the US Congress; it also affected lives on western river steamboats.[15]

Boasting of the Bloody Deed

In May 1856, South Carolina congressman Preston Brooks caned Massachusetts senator Charles Sumner in the US Senate chamber. This episode illustrated—on a national level—how infractions of honor could lead to violence.

As Brooks, Sumner, and many Americans understood, the concept of honor framed many southerners' interactions with one another and marked their position in society. Honor encompassed one's evaluation of self. It also harbored the community's opinion of the individual based on how that person followed societal guidelines. In his book *Kentucky Justice, Southern Honor, and American Manhood,* historian James C. Klotter writes that "honor represents a set of external, ethical rules supported by a collective community consciousness, a group of principles of socially expected conduct that establish what actions should be taken under what conditions." When it came to a real or perceived insult or the questioning of a man's masculinity, the response could be formal or informal: either a planned, negotiated duel or an impromptu street fight. In many instances, especially when a man was insulted by someone from a lower class, honor called for an immediate response. Disgrace had to be confronted, or else, historian Bertram Wyatt-Brown notes in his landmark work *Southern Honor: Ethics and Behavior in the Old South*, the brand of being a coward would "haunt the bearer forever." The failure to meet a challenge or to defend one's honor "was inseparable from community evaluation of the individual" and led to "the stigma of shame." As historian John Mayfield has also written, honor was a "Homeric" value in which it was imperative "to affirm one's worth publicly and to resist, at any cost, threats to that reputation."[16]

Klotter adds that "honorable individuals most feared not death but public humiliation, as a betrayal of manhood and honor. Honor required courage; cowardice meant shame; insults could not be tolerated. Action must follow, for only blood could cleanse the stains of honor." Because one's honor had "to be protected at every cost," historian John Hope Franklin writes, a southern male had to "defend with his life the slightest suggestion of irregularity in his honesty or integrity." This meant that calling someone a liar was a grave offense. Therefore, when Stevens called Jones a liar and thief for having counterfeit money, the honor of Jones, the son of a planter, was trampled on by Stevens, a lower-class clerk. It was further ground down when Stevens physically removed Jones from the cabin. As historian Edward L. Ayers explains, "Southern violence was triggered only by a limited number of specific cues, particularly insult. And although an outsider might offend a Southerner, the insult had to be considered an intentional affront before it would provoke violence." Having the lower-class Stevens manhandle Jones and physically force the Mississippian out of the cabin was another dire offense. Not only had the lower-class clerk called Jones a liar but he had also called his masculinity into question by shoving him out of the room. For Jones, it was a gravely intentional offence, and the combination of honor, insult, class differences, and physical force, mixed with Jones's drunkenness, was an unstable mix that made this public humiliation unbearable. Therefore, for Jones, the southern honor code called for the Mississippian to take immediate action, which he did by shooting Stevens. Richard F. Hamm writes that "one of the precepts of honor was that a man must respond to a verbal insult by seeking an apology, or, if necessary, by violence." To the drunken Jones, however, no apology could remove the stain. Immediate and brutal force was the only resolution. Jones did, however, have other options. As Dickson D. Bruce explains, "One would not fight a social inferior as an equal, and the instrument of castigation had to be different: a horsewhip, perhaps, or one might decide . . . not to fight at all but merely to shoot a potential attacker down and be done with it." Although using a pistol may have been acceptable in cities across the South, Jones was not on the streets of Vicksburg, Atlanta, Richmond, Nashville, or Louisville. Instead, he was confined on the *Ohio Belle*, surrounded by passengers and crew. Not all of those on board were southerners who adhered to the precepts of honor. Instead, they embraced shipboard justice and the act of taking the law into their own hands.[17]

5

Not the First Man I've Killed

Stevens was dead and Jones was trapped on the boat, a smoking revolver in his hand. Seeking a way to escape, the Mississippian raced up to the hurricane deck, pursued by passengers and crew. According to Captain Sebastian, the second clerk, C. P. Riley, who later bludgeoned Sebastian's brother with a whiskey bottle, caught Jones, knocked him to the ground, and stomped on his face, "which caused his mouth to bleed." Although Jones still held his pistol, he did not try to shoot anyone else. He also did not try to get up. A writer for the *Cairo Weekly Times* contended that Jones knew that he had nowhere to go. "He said it was his intentions to get to the stern of the boat, jump overboard and drown himself," the newspaper wrote.[1]

Riley planned to do more than beat the Mississippian. He "was in the act of pitching him overboard, when others interfered" and stopped the clerk from drowning Jones. Chaos reigned. Passengers crowded in, calling for Jones to be drowned or hanged. Others wanted legal justice to prevail. Finally, after "much difficulty was experienced," the justice-minded people on board prevented Jones's summary execution. The *Cairo Weekly Times* reported that Matilda Heron was the one who saved the killer's life. "As soon as he was captured," the newspaper reported, "one end of a strong rope was placed around his neck and preparations were rapidly making to string him up, at the juncture. Miss Heron, the actress, who was on board appeared and made a strong appeal to them [on] behalf of the young man and insisted upon their turning him over to the laws of the country to be dealt with. His execution was abandoned." Although the celebrity and emotional appeal of a trained and experienced actress saved Jones, it was later claimed that the murderer was beaten and tortured by the passengers and crew. Because of Jones's later treatment, and because captured thieves and criminals were typically treated roughly aboard steamboats, the Mississippian was likely physically abused.[2]

Some reporters contended that Jones was searched and that a large sum of counterfeit money was found in his possession. This story, however, was probably spread to further vilify Jones to the public. Conversely, a passenger later claimed that the money Jones passed to the barber was not counterfeit. Instead, he said, it was a note from the Bank of West Tennessee. Stevens simply did not recognize the currency and, therefore, proclaimed it to be a forgery. In this claim, which tried to use class and southern honor culture as an excuse for Jones's killing of Stevens, it was said that Stevens's refusal to take Jones's money insulted the Mississippian by equating him with a low-class thief. Therefore, Jones called Stevens "a damned liar and a scoundrel" before shooting him. Captain Sebastian, however, later wrote that the Mississippian was trying to pass off a forged bill that was supposedly from the Bank of Shelbyville, Tennessee. Because of Jones's sordid past, which was later revealed to the public, it is likely that the murderer was funding his steamboat journey with counterfeit money.[3]

The pleas of Heron and the other passengers who called for justice were answered. Jones's life, as the mob on the hurricane deck dropped their noose and dispersed, was spared. Jones was not, however, treated with kid gloves. The crew grabbed a rope to restrain him; if anyone knew how to tie knots, it was sailors. "He was taken abaft the shaft and lashed to a stancheon [sic]," a reporter wrote, "commencing with the rope at his feet and winding it around his body in continuous folds until it reached his neck, where it was drawn very tight. It was then passed around his head and across his mouth so tight that it stretched the corners of his mouth back considerably, cutting them so that the blood run [sic] down his jaws; and leaving him in the greatest agony." The crew would not lynch him, but they would use their rope skills to make the murderer of their fellow crewman suffer.[4]

Before being lashed below deck, Jones discussed the murder. He reiterated that he was J. B. Jones from Mississippi, and when he was told that Stevens was dead, he shrugged. "Well, I was drunk," he said. "He's not the first man I've killed." Jones's cavalier attitude excusing the murder because of drunkenness is not surprising. Edward Ayers writes that "alcohol and honor combined to create a volatile mixture." Ayers adds, "The cultural expectations of how drunken men are supposed to act obviously shape intoxicated behavior, and the Southern men who attacked companions or adversaries in drunken rage were acting in ways understandable, even expected, by others in their culture . . . Alcohol dissolved the barriers of self-restraint that kept honor under control." Although some would have understood Jones's drunken anger, others who embraced honor culture did not accept southern elites displaying rage and passion. Therefore, some newspapers downplayed Jones's supposed ties to the southern planter aristocracy, with one calling him "one of the many desperadoes and outlaws who infest our lower rivers."[5]

In addition to having a lax attitude about the murder, Jones exhibited the same outlook toward his own fate. He told the crew that he wanted to go to jail and face trial. If he was found guilty and sentenced to hang, then "he was willing to die." Others, however, claimed that "he never expected to reach Hickman, where the Captain of the Belle proposed to take him for trial." Jones's stoicism was yet another facet of southern honor culture. Because honor, as Dickson D. Bruce Jr. writes, was "focused heavily on projecting an image of self control," facing death calmly allowed Jones to present himself as a man of honor. He was able to drunkenly shrug off the killing of a lower-class clerk because, he believed, he was defending his honor. Moreover, by staring his potential execution squarely in the face, Jones was also trying to stake a claim to honor in the aftermath of the killing. In his book *The Kentucky Tragedy: A Story of Conflict and Change in Antebellum America*, Bruce examines one of the Bluegrass State's most famous honor killings, the murder of Solomon P. Sharp, a prominent legislator, by Jereboam Beauchamp. Beauchamp stabbed Sharp to death, in part, because of persistent rumors that Sharp had impregnated

Beauchamp's wife before the Beauchamps were married. When authorities sentenced Beauchamp to hang, the condemned man met his fate calmly. Like Beauchamp, Jones was, as Bruce writes, trying "to restore his public honor through courageously offering his life." If killing Stevens while intoxicated and full of rage and passion was dishonorable, then facing a trial and execution calmly was an attempt for Jones to restore any lost honor. This was, Bruce contends, "the highest realization of honor's demands."[6]

Although Jones staked a claim to honor by saying he would accept any legal fate, he also understood that he might never enter a courtroom. The Mississippian had nearly been lynched by the crew on the hurricane deck of the *Ohio Belle*. In addition to having this firsthand scrape with shipboard vigilantism, Jones had likely read newspaper accounts of steamboat workers dispensing their own form of riverine justice. As historian Louis C. Hunter explains, the "maintenance of law and order" aboard ships "devolved upon the captain." On western waters, however, and "in the spirit of the frontier," passengers and crew sometimes took the law into their own hands. Lawbreakers on steamboats could be flogged, whipped, or beaten before being placed ashore or left on an island in the river. Some had their heads shaved to brandish them as criminals, while others like Jones faced hanging or drowning at the hands of the crew.[7]

In 1841, for example, Edward Jarvis, a traveler on the Mississippi River, wrote in his diary about thieves creeping into staterooms to steal from wealthy passengers. "Last night such a fellow cut open the pantaloons on the abdomen six inches and the pocket of one of them fortunate fellows," Jarvis wrote, "and tried to get his money, but he was detected by the awakening of another who was by his side. Yesterday afternoon, two were detected stealing a coat and the Capt. set them on shore in the wilderness. This is the usual summary judgment and punishment of such fellows." In another incident on a different boat, three thieves had their heads shaved before being left on an island. They were, however, fortunate to not be aboard the *Chancellor*. In July 1853, as that steamboat traveled on the Mississippi River, several thieves were caught and tried on the boat. Five were sentenced to be whipped. It was evident that several of them had previously been punished in a similar manner. "Two of the five had their backs horribly lacerated by former floggings," a reporter wrote. In another incident on the *Woodford* in April 1857, an African American passenger "was terribly lynched" for theft. Earlier, when the *Germantown* caught fire on the Ohio River, some unscrupulous passengers used the chaos as an opportunity to rob the trunks of fellow travelers. Two of those men "were caught and lynched." Because newspapers sometimes conflated the word "lynched" with beatings or whippings, it is unknown if the men were killed or beaten.[8]

One of the most horrific episodes of steamboat lynch law occurred on the *Virginia* in 1855. On a voyage down the Mississippi River, the *Virginia* stopped at a wood yard just below Memphis to pick up fuel. There, a man was accused of stealing $60 from fellow travelers. The crew and some passengers tied the man up, took him to shore, shaved half of his head, stripped him, held him down, and then beat him with clubs for more than an hour. At one point during the ordeal, the man "begged" them to kill him. When one passenger complained about the ongoing brutality, he was told that he would share the same fate if he continued to object. Despite the beating—and although the accused man was near death—he never admitted to taking the passengers' money.[9]

Men who worked in the steamboat industry could also fall under the thrall of mob violence. Historian Zachary Bennett describes one instance where river workers' indolence, caused when steamboat traffic came to a standstill due to low river levels, erupted into something sinister. Bennett writes that in Cincinnati in the summer of 1841, when rumors spread that a black man had stabbed a white boy, "idle white river workers" raided an African American neighborhood. They "also destroyed the city's abolitionist newspaper by dragging its printing press into the Ohio's shallow waters." Among river men, anger over unemployment could spark mob rule and racial violence.[10]

When considering episodes of mob violence in river cities like Cincinnati, it is not surprising that mob-inspired vigilante justice occurred on steamboats. This conduct on the *Virginia*, the *Ohio Belle*, and other vessels was simply a reflection of behavior on land during this period. In fact, three episodes from the Ohio River city of Louisville are emblematic of how Americans embraced mob violence around the time that Jones killed Stevens on the *Belle*.

On November 2, 1853, Matthews Ward, the son of a prominent Louisville businessman and politician, shot and killed his brother's teacher, William Butler. The teacher had accused Ward's fifteen-year-old brother of lying before whipping him. When Matt Ward learned of the punishment, he believed that the discipline, administered by a lower-class teacher, insulted his younger brother, and, by extension, the Ward family. Therefore, the insult had to be addressed immediately. Matt went to Butler's school, argued with the teacher, slapped him, and then shot Butler in the chest in front of a group of students. Butler died the next day. Ward was arrested, and, after a change of venue, was tried for Butler's murder about forty miles from Louisville in Elizabethtown. Ward's family employed an incredible defense team of eighteen attorneys, including US senator John J. Crittenden. Thanks to this nineteenth-century "dream team," the jury acquitted Ward of the murder. This verdict infuriated Louisville residents. On hearing the result, nearly ten thousand people crammed the streets to condemn Ward, his family, and his legal team. The crowd met at the Jefferson County courthouse where they burned effigies of Ward, his attorney, and the jury. They then stormed over to Ward's father's house, an "elegant mansion," and pelted the home with stones. The rioters, it was reported, "demolished the beautiful and extensive glass conservatory, filled with rare plants and flowers, to the value of several thousand dollars; stoned and utterly destroyed the windows and window sashes, and wound up by setting the building on fire." The flames were extinguished, but the large, angry crowd illustrates how passions for mob violence were searing hot in 1850s America.[11]

A year after the jury acquitted Ward, mob violence again ran roughshod over Louisville. This time, however, politics and xenophobia drove the rioters. On August 6, 1855—as Louisville residents voted for governor, congressional representatives, and other offices—members of the American, or "Know Nothing," party attacked German and Irish citizens to prevent them from voting.

False rumors had spread that these foreign-born residents were hoarding weapons and preventing Know Nothing supporters from casting ballots. Single incidents of assault quickly exploded into mob violence as gangs of American Party members ransacked and burned immigrant-owned businesses, breweries, and homes. In the worst episode from what became known as "Bloody Monday," Know Nothing rioters burned down "Quinn's Row," a set of Irish-owned houses located in downtown Louisville. Those fleeing the flaming buildings were shot down. Although the true number of casualties is unknown, dozens died in what was Louisville's worst episode of nineteenth-century mob violence.[12]

Enslaved men and women accused of crimes also faced the wrath of mob-led vigilante violence. On December 18, 1856, four members of the white Joyce family were murdered in their cabin at Briar Creek, located fifteen miles from Louisville. The perpetrators bludgeoned the victims to death before setting the cabin ablaze. Among the dead was a three-year-old child, who was burned alive.

William Joyce, who lived in the cabin, returned home from a wedding to find the charred remains of his family. Suspecting foul play, several neighbors searched local farms for evidence. In one slave cabin they found watches, clothing, jewelry, and other items belonging to the Joyce family. The neighbors used violence to extricate a confession from Bill, the slave who lived in the cabin. Bill admitted that he and three other enslaved men murdered and stole from the Joyce family. The four slaves were seized, and, the *New Orleans Times-Picayune* reported, "they will probably be lynched." Many expected vigilante violence. The *Brooklyn Evening Star* wrote, "It was thought summary vengeance would be taken on the negroes."[13]

Although a mob hoped to kill the four slaves after their confession, cooler heads prevailed. Instead, the enslaved men were arrested and taken to Louisville for trial. During an examining trial there, however, William Joyce yelled, "Who ever is in favor of burning them, come on." Joyce tried to entice the crowd to attack, but they were restrained. Bill was the only slave who had confessed to the crime. The other three maintained their innocence, but one of the enslaved men was found in possession of "a hand axe dyed with blood."[14]

In May 1857, the four slaves were tried in Louisville. Bill, who became a witness for the state, was indicted for arson and robbery. The three other men were charged with arson, robbery, and murder. Much of the evidence was circumstantial; owing to a state law that disallowed uncorroborated testimony, Bill's accusations against his supposed co-conspirators were disregarded. The jury deliberated for only fifteen minutes. The slaves were acquitted.[15]

A large, seething crowd had gathered outside of the courthouse; therefore, the enslaved men were placed in a nearby jail to protect them. Soon, however, the enraged mob led by William Joyce descended on the jail. Some of the rioters looted a nearby arsenal, distributed muskets, and dragged a cannon to the front door of the jail. The mayor of Louisville tried to calm the crowd but was struck in the face by a brickbat and seriously injured. The mob and the police exchanged gunfire, and the jail was pelted with bricks and stones. As the crowd pressed forward, the jailer turned the slaves over to the mob. On being led out of his cell, one of the enslaved men slashed his own throat with a hidden razor and killed himself. The mob stepped over the dying man, seized the other three slaves, and hanged them in the courthouse yard. One of them struggled for more than ten minutes before dying. Two of the corpses were lit on fire.[16]

Some residents were horrified that yet again mob violence had engulfed Louisville. From the riots after the Ward trial to Bloody Monday and the lynching of the acquitted slaves, justice-minded citizens believed that law and order had been desecrated. The *Louisville Daily Courier* expressed this frustration. "Louisville was disgraced yesterday by another mob," the newspaper wrote, "which triumphantly rode over the laws, and satiated their vengeance . . . It is a fearful state of things, and conclusively shows the inefficiency of the public authorities." One resident contended that William Joyce and the other mob leaders would not be punished for carrying out vigilante justice. This was because "we are afraid of a ten fold more serious riot" and that "the general sympathy appears to be with him and his friends." Joyce and nine others were eventually arrested for inciting the lynching, but the charges were dismissed. The owners of the four dead slaves sued the city for their lost property, claiming $1,500 for the value of each murdered man. As these incidents illustrate, many Louisville residents were primed for mob violence and vigilante justice.[17]

Mob rule was not, of course, isolated to Louisville. As historian Leslie Ann Harper writes, "Mob violence occurred frequently in nineteenth-century America." In her study of the Bloody Monday riots, Harper notes that from 1828 to 1861, there were "403 riots against white targets in the southern United States" in which "criminals," "insurrectionists," and "abolitionists" were attacked. Moreover, as Dickson D. Bruce explains, the lynching of criminals was seen "as a product of frontier conditions in which law was not yet established." Bruce adds, however, that lynching criminals was typically applied "only when normal procedures failed."[18]

With riots and vigilantism having made headlines, and with passengers and crew recognizing that "normal procedures" related to justice would be difficult to find at a port downriver far from the scene of the crime, any fears Jones may have had about being lynched on the *Ohio Belle* were well-founded. By the time the *Belle* reached Cairo, Illinois, however, Jones was alive and tied firmly to pipes below deck. It appeared that he had escaped the vigilantes' noose or a watery grave.[19]

The town of Cairo, located where the Ohio River empties into the Mississippi, was a prominent stopping point for river traffic. On his 1841 journey, however, Edward Jarvis held out little hope for the town's success. "Here are some large warehouses," Jarvis wrote,

> for commission and storage and forwarding, one very large brick steam engine factory and iron foundry, one large building, probably for work shops, some fifty or more houses, some pretty, most all white. The town fronting on the Ohio and on a side running northward from [the Mississippi] is enclosed with a high levee, so high that we could only see the roofs of some low houses beyond it. There is a hope of business in this enclosed swamp, and it is said that some millions of dollars have been expended to raise a city here. But it seems to me a fruitless work.[20]

The *Belle* reached Cairo at noon, only about an hour after Jones had killed Stevens. With the Mississippian bound below deck, Captain Sebastian left the boat, went into town, and procured a coffin for Stevens's body. Sebastian also sent several crew members to talk to an attorney about leaving Jones in Cairo to be tried for murder. According to Sebastian, the lawyer told them "that in all probability the court would discharge Jones for want of jurisdiction if I left him at Cairo." It is also likely that some passengers and crew knew that if Jones were turned over to authorities for trial, he might be acquitted for killing Stevens. As Dickson Bruce writes, an "understandable fit of passion" could sometimes lead to an acquittal. When one man killed another while full of rage, Bruce explains, judges and jurors often believed that they "could not therefore be guilty of malicious, premeditated murder. It was an argument defense attorneys would make throughout the antebellum period" and could "mitigate the crime." Many southerners believed, Bruce notes, that acting "violently implied a provocation so extreme that the individual himself could no longer exercise control over his actions—and, it was only such a loss of control that made violence understandable." This is one reason why Jones was willing to be turned over to authorities to face trial. In addition to getting him away from a vengeful crew, he also knew that he had a good chance of getting acquitted if he claimed self-defense or that he had acted out of extreme passion. In Matt Ward's widely publicized trial held before Jones killed Stevens, for example, Ward had been found not guilty of killing his brother's teacher. Because authorities in Cairo were reticent to prosecute Jones, Captain Sebastian decided to take the murderer to Hickman, Kentucky, for trial. Sebastian said that the *Belle* remained at Cairo until approximately five o'clock in the evening. During that time, it is likely that passengers and crew had thoughts similar to what President Andrew Jackson's mother supposedly told him: "The law affords no remedy that can satisfy the feelings of a true man."[21]

While docked at Cairo, Sebastian's wife, who was also on board, told her husband that the rope tied around Jones's neck had loosened and slipped down. She feared that Jones might accidentally hang himself, so Sebastian went below deck and changed the rope. Others claimed that "a lady," possibly Matilda Heron, "begged" the crew to provide Jones, who had been left standing tied to a stanchion bound head to foot, with more comfortable treatment. Regardless of who expressed concern, Sebastian took the upper part of the rope off, leaving Jones's arms and body bound. Since Jones was weary from being tied standing up, Sebastian put the Mississippian in a chair and fastened him "to the supply pipe . . . in the engine room at the after end of the boilers." This placed Jones in a location where the engineer could watch him. Sebastian tied Jones sitting down, with his arms and body bound to the supply pipe. "He was not tied to the chair," the captain wrote, "his feet were not tied together." Sebastian added that "the object was to keep him secure, not to torture him." The captain said that he would turn the killer over to authorities. "At the time of the murder there was very naturally a great deal of excitement among the passengers," Sebastian wrote, "as well as the crew, and I was fearful that some of them might take the law into their own hands, but this had apparently died away, and all on board seemed to be satisfied with the conclusion to deliver Jones to the proper authorities at Hickman." When he left Jones, he believed that the passengers and crew had lost their taste for vigilante justice.[22]

The *Ohio Belle* remained in Cairo for nearly five hours so that Sebastian could make arrangements for Stevens's remains. The captain hired the Adams Express Company to ship the clerk's body to Cincinnati. Another officer from the *Belle* accompanied Stevens on his final journey. Stevens was buried at Spring Grove Cemetery[23] in Cincinnati on March 17, three days after his death. "His funeral was attended by the Odd Fellows and Red Men," the *Evansville Daily Journal* wrote. "All the steamers at the Cincinnati wharf had their flags at half-mast, in token of respect to the deceased . . . He was an excellent business man and generally esteemed." The *Cincinnati Commercial* noted that Stevens's funeral was held at the residence of Captain Henry A. Jones on Pike Street in Cincinnati. Jones was the steamboat captain and entrepreneur who had briefly commanded the first and second iterations of the *Ohio Belle*. He was also a part owner of the vessel. The *Commercial* added that "the large attendance fully attested the high respect with which the deceased was regarded by the community." The murdered man was married with four children.[24]

While the *Belle* was at Cairo, passengers and crew mulled over what to do with Jones, who remained tied below deck. As Stevens's body was carried off the vessel, the crew surely discussed Cairo authorities' unwillingness to prosecute the murder. Furthermore, one reporter wrote, "the passengers were canvassing the propriety of hanging him without further ceremony." Sebastian's assessment of having calm, justice-minded travelers on board was inaccurate. Moreover, the delay at Cairo made those on board restless. It also allowed word of the murder to spread onto shore. At one point, some Cairo residents tried to shove their way on board in order to hang Jones, but the crew prevented the lynching. It was also reported, however, that the crowd was, in fact, trying to save Jones, because they learned that the crew had planned on killing him after the murder. They feared for Jones's life once the *Belle* left town. This version of the story is more likely because the crew probably would have turned the Mississippian over to an angry lynch mob and joined in the execution. When the group of well-meaning residents appeared at the wharf, however, the *Belle* had already pulled out into the river. Whatever their intent (trying to save the murderer from mob rule was likely, considering that the crew would have joined any lynching party), Jones's fate was out of their hands.[25]

On leaving Cairo, the *Ohio Belle* steamed down the Mississippi River, heading toward Hickman. After traveling twelve miles, the boat stopped at a wood yard to load fuel. The *Belle* remained there for an hour and a half. The passengers ate dinner during the delay, and at this stop, it is likely that a group—either passengers, crew, or a combination of the two—hatched an idea for how to deal with the Mississippian. Their plan would be executed before the *Belle* reached Hickman.[26]

After the boat left the wood yard, Sebastian went to the pilot house to supervise the evening journey. At eight thirty, twenty-five miles above Hickman, a crew member appeared and told the captain that Jones was missing. Sebastian said that he could not leave the pilot house because he had to guide the vessel. Therefore, he instructed the crew to search for the prisoner. They scoured the ship, but the Mississippian was nowhere to be found. Jones had disappeared.[27]

When Sebastian learned that the crew had failed to find the killer, he went below deck to investigate. "The fastenings had been cut," he wrote, "the ends of the line showing this plainly, and the chair on which Jones had been sitting was gone." Because Matilda Heron had been concerned for Jones's safety, and because passengers and crew still whispered about lynching Jones before the *Belle* reached Hickman, some believed that the actress had severed the cords to allow Jones to jump overboard and swim to safety. Others contended that Jones's disappearance was a suicide or that he had drowned while trying to escape. Sebastian said that because the *Belle* was laden with goods, he believed that Jones was hiding on board among the freight. Once the boat docked, the captain contended, the Mississippian would slip from his hiding place and try to evade capture. Curiously, at the time of Jones's disappearance, Sebastian said that "the engineer had stepped aft to examine . . . the main shaft, [and] when he returned to his station at the engines the prisoner was gone." The editor of the *New Orleans Daily Crescent* was puzzled over the incident, reporting that "the rope by which the chair had been fastened was cut, and both chair and occupant had disappeared. What became of the murderer no one pretended to know."[28]

The *Ohio Belle* reached Hickman, where Sebastian had planned to leave Jones with local authorities. Interestingly, the boat spent little time there, with no one speaking with authorities or looking for the murderer. Instead, and with the crew showing little concern for the escaped killer, and after loading and unloading freight and passengers, the *Belle* departed. As the vessel pulled back into the river, one officer reputedly said that "they need not be surprised if they find a dead man floating there about." Another claimed that Sebastian yelled, "If you find a damned scoundrel floating by on a chair, take him out and hang him!"[29]

Shortly thereafter, bobbing near a sandbar in the river near Hickman, a drowned man, dressed in fashionable yet shabby clothes, was found tied to a chair. It was Jones.[30]

6

A Man of Property

News of Jones's death spread quickly. The *Louisville Daily Courier* remarked that it "excited much comment," while another publication said that Jones was "drowned like a dog!" Others speculated that the boat's officers had ordered Jones's death, and that "an effort would be made to arrest them."[1]

After Stevens's murder, newspapers were sympathetic to the dead clerk's comrades on the *Ohio Belle*. When news broke that Jones's body had been discovered, however, the press condemned Sebastian and the crew. The *Louisville Daily Courier*, which had reported that Jones had "foully murdered" Stevens, wrote that the Mississippian was found "at the head of the bar below Hickman, lashed to the chair in precisely the same manner that he was tied on the steamboat." They lambasted the crew, adding that "Jones was thrown overboard and drowned with the knowledge and connivance of the officers of the boat." The *Richmond Daily Dispatch* was horrified at those who had pitched Jones into the water. "Tied fast to a chair," their reporter wrote, "his arms pinioned, Jones was thrown overboard, and thus died without being able to make a struggle for his life; and this was done, too, by men who call themselves human!" Others called for justice. A St. Louis newspaper wrote that they and other journalists "severely denounce the officers of the boat for permitting this barbarous act to be perpetrated. We hope all concerned in the outrage, may be severely punished." The *Memphis Eagle* simply said that Jones was "foully dealt with." In the midst of this coverage, the focus changed from Stevens's murder to the vigilante execution of J. B. Jones.[2]

From Missouri, Indiana, Kentucky, and beyond, questions arose about the crew's involvement in Jones's death. "The impression throughout this part of the country is," a western Kentucky newspaper wrote, "that a most horrible murder has been perpetrated by the officers and crew of the boat." Although Stevens's death had elicited sympathy, those on the *Ohio Belle* were now called a "murderous crew."[3]

With the Mississippian's demise, regional mores and class prejudice influenced the way many regarded the crew and their alleged treatment of Jones. When southern writers realized that Jones was the son of a Mississippi planter and part of the region's elite, sympathy for Stevens evaporated. Many contended that an innocent and misunderstood Jones, who shot Stevens because he had been insulted and was defending his honor, had been mistreated and murdered by the coarse sailors who worked on the *Ohio Belle*. The public understood the reputation of riverboat workers, and some began to question if Jones had really tried to pass counterfeit bills. Those bowing to the planter aristocracy defended Jones and accused the crew of killing him for his money. "The impression throughout this part of the country is, that a most horrible murder has been perpetrated by the officers and crew of the boat," one editor wrote. "Mr. Jones was a respectable man, a citizen of Mississippi, we believe, and a man of property. We have not learned what became of the money which he had with him. He certainly did not take it with him when he 'jumped overboard.'" The paper continued by blaming Stevens, the victim, who surely must have insulted the gentlemanly Jones. "Whilst we admit that he laid himself liable to punishment by shooting the clerk, we must say that almost any man of spirit having been grossly insulted and finally assaulted [pushed out of the cabin by Stevens], would have done the same thing." Because southern honor culture called for a dishonored gentleman to immediately respond with violence against an insult from a lower-class man, the newspaper justified Jones's slaying of Stevens based on the code of honor.[4]

As the story spread, and as accusations piled up against the crew of the *Ohio Belle*, Sebastian published his own version of events. Written in Cincinnati on April 10, 1856, and widely circulated, it was called "a true statement of the whole affair." By writing it, the captain hoped to absolve himself and his crew of murder. Sebastian called the entire tragedy "a deplorable affair." He also singled out the *Memphis Bulletin*, which was one of the first newspapers to charge the crew with murdering Jones. Sebastian said that their claims were "untrue." The captain added that "it is strange that a respectable newspaper will, under the impulse of the moment, give currency and credit to reports so injurious to any one, without being entirely satisfied of their truth." Sebastian added his own pinch of honor culture into the brew, writing that "the editor or conductor of a paper cannot be too careful, as a mere incidental remark in the editorial columns may be the source of great injustice; and deliberate charges so may carry with them so much of authority, that a man may be ruined by them without the chance of redress." Because southern gentlemen seeking violent, physical "redress" had previously attacked newspaper editors due to articles that they had written, the captain's meaning was clear. Sebastian concluded his card by noting that "those who know me will bear testimony to my character as a law abiding man, and all who were on the Ohio Belle at the time will exonerate me from the charge of a desire to execute lynch law on the murderer of Stevens." Several papers, including those in Louisville, the city of Sebastian's birth, believed that the article proved that Sebastian was "wholly ignorant of the manner and time of the disappearance of the passenger." They contended that he had nothing to do with Jones's murder. Authorities and newspapers located near Jones's native Mississippi, however, were not so convinced.[5]

The Memphis press, publishing their work about fifteen miles from the Mississippi border, were among those who made excuses for the murderer. They called Jones "a respectable man" who was surely "a man of property." They wrote as if they *knew* him, but they did not. For the dead man tied to a chair bobbing in the waves by the sandbar near Hickman was not really named J. B. Jones.

His real name was Joseph Cocke Jr. Although his clothes were shabby and "Jones" was an alias, his mannerisms—touchiness

The *Memphis Eagle* reported that Joseph Cocke Sr. was "a most worthy gentleman residing near Holly Springs, Mississippi." The newspaper praised him, despite the fact that his son had killed his friend William J. Sanderson on the streets of the town.

bred by southern honor culture—and an attitude befitting the son of a wealthy Mississippi planter were not an act. He was indeed the offspring of, the *Memphis Eagle* reported, "a most worthy gentleman residing near Holly Springs, Mississippi." Moreover, while his upbringing and ancestry may have been worthy, his past was deeply disturbing.[6]

When newspapers learned about Jones's true family ties, they double-downed on tales that Stevens had provoked Cocke. Because Cocke came from an honorable family, he was therefore an honorable man. Jones, newspapers argued, was revealed to be a true man of honor, hailing from the prominent Cockes of Holly Springs. Therefore, he had to have been assaulted by the lower-class clerk. As a purported gentleman—regardless of his past, his inebriation, or the fact that he lied and lived under an assumed name—these southern newspapers reported, Cocke would not have attacked Stevens without provocation. Furthermore, because Cocke was born into a wealthy family, the money in his pocket could not have been counterfeit. This was claimed even when it was revealed that the murderous Cocke had been on the run from the law.

Southern honor culture entangled with class prejudice influenced the changing tide of public opinion about Cocke's murder of Stevens. Memphis is less than fifty miles from Cocke's hometown of Holly Springs, and editors in that Tennessee town who likely knew, or at least wanted to impress Cocke's family, were quick to rush to the murderer's defense. When Cocke's father traveled through Memphis while on his way to retrieve his son's body, the *Memphis Eagle* called the drowned murderer "ill-fated" and said that "we sincerely sympathize with the father and family of the unfortunate and unhappy youth, of whom it may be truly said—'After life's fitful fever he sleeps well.'" For these editors, condemnation of Stevens's killer had ended. Instead, they rushed to the defense of the high-bred murderer, Cocke.[7]

In his study *Violence and Culture in the Antebellum South*, Dickson D. Bruce writes that many southerners believed that "the elite, the 'aristocracy,' with their manners and their training, were far less likely to commit acts of violence than were people who lacked the requisite breeding . . . Class was, after all, more a matter of behavior than of money." Therefore, newspapers assumed that the lower-class clerk surely insulted, abused, or impugned the honor of Cocke, or else the Mississippian would not have reacted with impetuous, unchecked passion. This argument placed Stevens's murder squarely on his own shoulders.[8]

The man whom these newspapers excused was indeed a man of means and property. Cocke's father, Joseph Cocke Sr.—born in Campbell County, Virginia, on June 12, 1798—was a wealthy planter who lived just outside of Holly Springs in Marshall County, Mississippi. In 1850, Joseph Sr. owned twenty-one enslaved African Americans, thirteen men and eight women, ranging in ages from one to thirty-five years. After his son's death, Joseph Sr.'s wealth continued to grow. In 1860, for example, he owned thirty-five slaves, twenty-four men, and eleven women. Ten years earlier, his twenty-one-year-old, Tennessee-born son, Joseph Jr.— later to die under the pseudonym "Jones"—was living on his father's plantation and working as a farmer. Joseph Jr.'s three sisters, ages fourteen, twelve, and eight, also lived there. The young Joseph also had an elder brother, George Washington Cocke, who was becoming a wealthy farmer in his own right. The family lived surrounded by other members of the planter aristocracy in their corner of Marshall County.[9]

With this wealth came political activity. In August 1851, Joseph Sr. was one of several vice presidents on a committee organizing a "Davis Barbecue" in Holly Springs to honor Mississippi politician and future Confederate president Jefferson Davis. Joseph Sr. had long been involved in Magnolia State Democratic politics. In 1845, for example, he helped choose delegates to the Marshall County Democratic convention.[10]

In 1851 the twenty-two-year-old Joseph Jr. made a decision that altered his fate and destroyed his status as an honorable man. That December, he was engaged to marry a girl from Holly Springs. In order to "test" the faithfulness (or honor) of his fiancée, Joseph Jr. enlisted his friend, a twenty-four-year-old Virginia-born farmer named William J. Sanderson, "to address this young lady himself." When Sanderson called on the young woman, instead of helping his friend, Sanderson offered his own proposal. Joseph Jr.'s fiancée accepted, and Sanderson and the woman were soon married. Twenty minutes after their wedding ceremony, Joseph Jr. asked Sanderson to step outside. There, on the streets of Holly Springs, Joseph Jr. shot Sanderson in the face. "The bullet penetrated the brain," the *New Orleans Daily Crescent* reported. Another newspaper wrote that "the ball [struck] the chin and [ranged] up into his head, causing his death in a few minutes." When Sanderson fell, Joseph Jr. jumped on his horse and fled. There, amid the black powder smoke, trampling hooves, blood, and cries of a young bride, J. B. Jones was born.[11]

In the aftermath of Sanderson's murder, the *Holly Springs Jeffersonian* bemoaned the fact that a good family had been tarnished. "A mournful event has occurred in our town," they wrote, "and our citizens have again been startled with a violent death in their midst. With pain and reluctance we record the affair. A worthy and distressed family must be tortured by a public announcement of a deed of blood committed by a Son and Brother. Upon our town must rest the stigma of the commission of such a deed in it, and the escape of a man charged with the commission of the deed."[12]

A grand jury investigated the shooting and charged Cocke with "willful murder." The victim's elder brother, the twenty-eight-year-old planter David D. Sanderson, offered a $500 reward for Cocke's capture. David was also a member of the region's planter elite. By 1860 he had amassed $20,000 in real estate, $30,000 in his personal estate, and twenty-six enslaved African Americans, ages two to fifty-two. The governor of Mississippi added a $200 reward for Cocke's capture, but the killer remained on the run, with some claiming that he had fled to Cuba. From time to time, before Cocke killed Stevens on the *Ohio Belle,* rumors spread that he had been captured. In 1854, for example, it was claimed that the Mississippian had been arrested in Richmond, Virginia. This rumor was also reported in the *New York Herald,* the *Washington Daily Union,* and several other newspapers. The Mississippian, however, would not surface again until he killed Hiram Stevens on the *Ohio Belle.*[13]

Although newspapers knew that Cocke had killed Sanderson, blinded by class prejudice they blamed Stevens for provoking his own murder. In their eyes, Cocke was a gentleman because of his birth and family wealth. Gentlemen, however, did not act with unbridled passion, as Cocke had done when he murdered both Sanderson and Stevens. Todd Hagstette writes that "free indulgence in emotions—especially anger, hatred, and aggression—became the mark of ungentlemanly behavior." Dickson D. Bruce concurs, noting that "being a gentleman required an ability to act with restraint; the man who could not was unfit to demand the respect due to someone of stature."[14]

This is why duels were negotiated and fought within a highly formalized structure—they were kept stylized in order to keep the participants dispassionate. One witness to a 1798 affair of honor wrote that "in well-bred Society, when a man receives an affront, does he knock down the person giving it? No. He represses his feelings; and takes another time and place to obtain justice."

Although white southerners were raised to avoid, as Bruce calls it, "the dangers of passion," by killing Sanderson and Stevens, Cocke embraced his anger and acted out of rage. Although alcohol surely stoked Cocke's reaction on the *Ohio Belle*, the fact that he lived under an assumed name, killed his newly wed friend, and reacted with imperious, arrogant spontaneity and without self-restraint, erased his claims to being honorable. Yet southern newspapers believed that Stevens had wronged him, so violence was acceptable. This details a class distinction within the structure of southern honor culture; although acting with passion against Sanderson was condemned and ungentlemanly because Sanderson was a social equal (Cocke should have instead issued his friend a challenge to duel), newspapers excused the murder of Stevens because the clerk was from a lower class. Such were the class-sensitive distinctions of southern honor culture. The spontaneous killing of an equal made Cocke a murderer, whereas the impulsive shooting of a steamboat clerk brought Cocke some sympathy. Again, as that newspaper proclaimed, "almost any man of spirit having been grossly insulted and finally assaulted would have done the same thing."[15]

Although gentlemen planters were expected to keep their actions dispassionate, their society encouraged many of them to act imperiously and impetuously. John Randolph could have been writing about Cocke when he described some fellow southerners. "A petulant arrogance . . . marks the character of too many of our young men. They early assume airs of manhood; and these premature men remain children for the rest of their lives . . . placed in the society of *real* gentlemen, and men of letters, they are awkward and uneasy: in all situations, they are contemptible." Part of this puerile behavior was reacting with a hair-trigger when insulted.[16]

For the sons of the plantation elite like Cocke, slavery influenced their touchiness, arrogance, and reliance on honor. Richard F. Hamm writes that honor was "intertwined" with slavery, whereas Dickson Bruce notes that the peculiar institution "brought violence into the planter home . . . the violence of slavery, as an example, proved that white Southerners, men and women, did recognize a place for violence in dealings with other people." From childhood games to hunting to disciplining slaves, Cocke and other southerners were introduced to violence at an early age. Bruce adds that southern children "learned to turn to violence only when no other course of action seemed available, only when they were backed to the wall. The problem was, of course, that they could become backed to the wall rather quickly." This was especially true of upper-class southerners. One man who visited South Carolina in 1839 said that children lording over enslaved people at an early age provided "the foundation of that irascible temper and ungovernable self-will, which characterize nearly all the white inhabitants of the Slave States."[17]

The prevalence of concealed weapons also drove violence. Because planters lived in fear of slave uprisings and, therefore, constantly carried weapons, the institution created a paranoia that led to an armed society. "The planter regarded arms as a necessary adjunct to the machinery of control," Franklin writes. Moreover, he adds, "Arming themselves with knives and guns became habitual with some masters and overseers. In moments of anger, they sometimes turned their weapons against each other. This was to be expected among an aggregation of armed lords having no superimposed discipline." If alcohol was mixed with cultural touchiness and concealed weapons, tragedy could result, as in the case of Cocke shooting Stevens on board the *Ohio Belle*.[18]

Cocke epitomized the sensitive, arrogant, planter's son who wore concealed weapons and bore a heightened awareness toward insult. As a member of the elite who played a hand in controlling his father's slaves, he was contemptuous toward those who questioned him and was used to getting his way. And when others did not conform to his wishes—whether he was jilted by a friend or questioned and manhandled by a steamboat clerk—he responded with violence. He was not genteel. Instead he had what Dickson Bruce calls "cocksure impetuosity," full of anger, passion, and petulant rage. "Ever ready to see a threat at the hands of others," Bruce writes in *Violence and Culture in the Antebellum South,* "a Southern man might be prepared, as well, to punish any attacker who should appear." In another study, Bruce notes that "people enraptured with honor saw the world as a hostile place in which threats were everywhere and in which one needed always to be prepared to respond." This touchiness condemned both Sanderson and Stevens.[19]

Cocke's membership in the "touch-wood gentry" also meant that he condemned himself. In killing a crew member on a steamboat, those on board who felt no compunction to bow to Cocke's stature, bound him to a chair and threw him into the river to drown.

This act of vigilante justice led to accusations of murder. Grand juries in western Kentucky counties along the Mississippi River began investigating "Jones's" death. Because witnesses were spread across the region, including passengers from different states as well as transient crew members, grand juries had difficulty procuring testimony. Sebastian, still working on the river, let his published defense stand for itself. The *Louisville Daily Courier* wrote, "If Sebastian is the upright man that he wishes by his late publication to make the public believe he is, let him come forward and permit a fair legal investigation of the whole affair." Although Sebastian spoke little about the incident, he was apparently wary of legal action. On trips downriver after Cocke's execution, the *Ohio Belle* avoided stops in Hickman, Paducah, and Smithland, where local authorities were evidently poised to arrest the captain and some crew members. Despite the difficulty of finding cooperative witnesses, in April 1856, the grand jury of Ballard County, Kentucky, indicted Sebastian for Cocke's murder.[20]

The indictment stopped neither Sebastian nor the *Ohio Belle* from working the rivers. In May 1856, the crew transported thousands of pounds of marble to Evansville, Indiana, and "a large amount of sugar and molasses" to Louisville. Sebastian remained free, commanding the *Belle*. In June he attended a meeting in Louisville with other steamboat captains to discuss possible improvements to the Falls of the Ohio. Four months later, he and Captain R. M. Wade inspected enhancements made to the Ohio River canal in Louisville. The murders of Stevens and Cocke did not dampen merchants' interest in using the *Belle* and did not hinder their faith in Sebastian. In December 1856, the *Daily Louisville Times* wrote that "the Belle is one of the best Cincinnati boats, and is commanded by that clever gentleman, John Sebastian, and at her desk is her musical Clerk, formerly a member of the Steinetta Troupe [who likely replaced the slain Stevens]. Passengers going South, may rest assured that they will be well taken care of and luxuriously entertained on the Ohio Belle." By June 1857, Sebastian still commanded the vessel.[21]

Although the lavish surroundings of the *Belle* continued to impress, the steamer did encounter some problems. In March 1857, the vessel "broke a side pipe" near Evansville, Indiana, and had to travel upriver "on one wheel." On the same trip, the *Belle* got hung up at the Portland Canal and became stuck on rocks on the Falls of the Ohio. The crew had to bring in equipment to pull the vessel from the obstacle. A month later, on a downriver trip to New Orleans, three thieves boarded the boat at Memphis. After they robbed several passengers' staterooms, the boat's watchman (onboard security) caught one of the thieves, grabbed him by the collar, and ripped it. Although the thief initially escaped, he was later recognized because of his torn collar. He and the other two robbers were caught. With the vigilante execution of Cocke having occurred on the boat under the same captain, one would think that thieves would avoid the *Ohio Belle.* Perhaps the bandits did not read the newspapers; regardless, they picked the wrong crew to bother. "They had robbed several passengers," a reporter wrote, "but were made to disgorge their ill-gotten gains. They were then pretty roughly treated, and their heads shaved, and then put ashore on an Island in the Mississippi." If Cocke's fate was any indication, their larceny on board the *Belle* carried a risk that they were fortunate to avoid.[22]

In early 1858, Sebastian went on trial for Cocke's murder. The case had been delayed several times, likely because key witnesses had been difficult to find. During the proceedings, one passenger stated that Sebastian "knew nothing whatever of the disappearance of the man." Eventually, all charges were dropped for lack of evidence. It remains unclear if the crew, passengers, or a mixture of the two were the ones who perpetrated vigilante justice on Stevens's killer. But, Sebastian was set free.[23]

The *Queen of the West* was one of several steamboats, including the *Ohio Belle*, that joined the Cincinnati and New Orleans Express Packet Line. These vessels were "furnished equal to a first-class hotel." (Public Library of Cincinnati and Hamilton County)

The charges and trial did little to diminish Sebastian's reputation or workload. In fact, in November 1858, the *Ohio Belle* joined the "Cincinnati and New Orleans Express Packet Line" with nine other boats, including the *Monarch, Tecumseh, Switzerland, Susquehanna, Queen of the West,* and others. Emerson Gould, an early Mississippi River historian, wrote that the boats comprising this line were "known as short boats, and could pass the locks in the Louisville canal—were not fast, but of large carrying capacity, with fine accommodations for passengers, and their tables were furnished equal to a first-class hotel." He added that they kept to a schedule and that "their regularity, promptness and good management was such an improvement upon the former style of running Cincinnati boats engaged in the New Orleans trade, that they soon secured a popularity that promised very satisfactory results."[24]

Sebastian commanded the *Belle* during the boat's tenure with the Cincinnati and New Orleans Express Packet Line. In late February 1859, it was reported that the *Belle, Aurora,* and *Mars* passed by Cairo on the way to New Orleans. Although the rivers were still busy with steamboats, the expansion of railroad lines was negatively affecting their business. "The Aurora was loaded to the guards," the *Cincinnati Daily Press* reported. "The other two were not well loaded." The next several years witnessed the rapid decline of the steamboat era. But in mid-March at least, the *Belle* and *Mars* reached Cincinnati from New Orleans, "fully freighted."[25]

Despite the advent of rail transportation, the *Ohio Belle* continued to deliver an array of goods between Cincinnati and New Orleans. In March 1860, the steamboat took a load to Ohio that included bacon, hams, sixty-six barrels of onions, 108 barrels of potatoes, fifty boxes of cheese, three hundred boxes of candles, ten boxes of sausages, thirty-six barrels of alcohol, twelve barrels of whiskey, hundreds of empty kegs, butter, flour, beef, thirty reels of yarn, wine, crackers, furniture, beer, tobacco, plows, and more. Several months later, another northward delivery included butter, apples, celery, eggs, pigs' feet, beef tongues, pork shoulders, ribs, lard, cabbage, oil, malt, lime, and other "sundries."[26]

Although the *Belle* had previously treated the criminal element roughly, some passengers still boarded the vessel with nefarious intentions. In December 1859, for example, a passenger named John Ryan was sent to the New Orleans workhouse for six months "for stealing a box of candles from the cargo of the steamer Ohio Belle." With sectional tensions rising across the nation, however, the crew of the *Belle,* who made their living on the trade and passenger business between the north and south, soon had much more to worry about than a pilfered box of candles.[27]

7

Oh! The Horrors of War

When the enslaved Samuel Watson shook his attorney's hand and bade him farewell, the Ohio River again became a highway leading him to perpetual bondage. The same held true for Margaret Garner and her baby, Cilla, on the *Henry Lewis*, steaming toward Arkansas and a continued life of toil. It was a fate so appalling that Garner tossed her infant into the river to keep the child from enslavement.

The men and women who watched these incidents unfold, from Matilda Heron and John Sebastian passing by the submerged *Henry Lewis*, to Salmon P. Chase cradling the silver pitcher given to him by the Baker Street Church, soon saw the Union crumble over slavery. Chase, who became President Abraham Lincoln's secretary of the treasury, witnessed the turmoil of the national collapse more closely than most. Nevertheless, all Americans were affected as the nation split apart, including those involved with the *Ohio Belle*, which played its own role in the subsequent conflict.

When the Civil War erupted, the *Ohio Belle*, owned by Sebastian and investors Thomas Sherlock, Henry A. Jones, and C. G. Pearce, continued to work the rivers. Despite the threat of war, this "staunch and regular passenger packet" continued hauling trade and people along its route between Cincinnati and New Orleans. Although the *Belle* was an Ohio-owned boat, by the time Louisiana and other states in the Deep South had seceded from the Union, the vessel still delivered passengers and goods to New Orleans. Trade continued between the contending regions. Before one trip, however, a small fire erupted on the *Belle*. Although the blaze was "easily extinguished," it portended bad tidings for the steamboat.[1]

On April 15, 1861, the *Belle* was docked at Evansville, Indiana, loading freight for another trip to Louisiana. Three days earlier, Southern forces in South Carolina fired on the Union garrison at Fort Sumter in Charleston Harbor. The fort surrendered the next day. While the *Belle* waited at Evansville, President Abraham Lincoln called for seventy-five thousand troops to crush the rebellion. Texas had seceded in February, joining Louisiana and six other states, and Lincoln's call for soldiers pushed Virginia to leave the Union on April 17. Arkansas, North Carolina, and Tennessee soon followed. Despite the fractured Union, the *Belle* continued its voyage southward, reaching New Orleans on April 21.[2]

Although the trip downriver was initially peaceful, when the boat unloaded freight at New Orleans the crew found themselves swept up in the conflict. Upstream, events were spiraling out of control. Secessionists in Memphis were raising troops and had blocked the Mississippi River. "The excitement in this city is at a high pitch," a newspaper wrote. Pro-Confederate residents knew that the *Ohio Belle,* the *Mars,* and two other ships were soon leaving New Orleans for the return journey north. They planned to seize those Yankee-owned vessels for the good—and the honor—of the South. The *Shreveport Daily News* noted that "the steamers Ohio Belle and Monarch are still below this point, and if they reach Cincinnati without being overhauled, it will be because our sentinels sleep at their post—a probability that is useless to be entertained." Sadly for the *Belle*, few were slumbering.[3]

Unionists and secessionists along the river were playing a game of retribution: you seize my property and I'll take yours. In May 1861, residents of Cairo, Illinois, confiscated $175,000 worth of weapons bound for Tennessee when they captured the steamer *C. E. Hillman*. In response, Volunteer State secessionists planned to detain the *Ohio Belle* and other Northern-owned vessels until reparations were made. Tennesseans, however, were foiled by their allies. Zealous rebels in Arkansas instead claimed the prize.[4]

As vessels along the Mississippi River fell into Southern hands,

At the beginning of the Civil War, secessionist residents of Napoleon, Arkansas, seized the *Ohio Belle*. The steamboat was then pressed into Confederate service until it was recaptured by Union forces.

the *Ohio Belle* left New Orleans, bound for home. The boat arrived in Napoleon, Arkansas, on April 29. Twenty years earlier, steamboat passenger Edward Jarvis described the town while he rode up the Mississippi. "Napoleon is the stopping place at the mouth of this river," he wrote, "where passengers and goods get out for a change of boats. Napoleon is a bit of a place with a dozen or two houses, two or three larger ware and store houses shut up, two or three small stores, a hotel or two, and in all a disagreeable-looking place." The crew of the *Belle*, paranoid about their safety during the northward journey, wanted to quickly depart this small town, which had not changed much since Jarvis passed by.[5]

They had reason to worry. Several weeks earlier, Cincinnati residents had seized arms, ammunition, and four cannon intended for secessionist forces in Arkansas. That state's governor, Henry M. Rector, was incensed. He blamed the confiscation on "the people of Cincinnati having instinctive proclivities towards public plunder." Determined to avenge the Queen City's insult, Rector ordered troops to snatch all Cincinnati-owned steamboats, including the *Ohio Belle* and the *Mars*. This would be done, Rector said, "to secure them and their cargoes against waste or damage until restitution should be made of the property captured in Cincinnati." Citizens of Napoleon took this order to heart. They gathered arms and posted several artillery pieces near the shore. A. C. Denson, who was in Napoleon at the time, wrote that "the citizens of Napoleon, Arkansas, had hoisted the Secession Flag, and were greatly excited about some powder and lead which had been taken by the United States' authorities at Cincinnati, while bound for the ports of Memphis and New Orleans." When the *Belle* arrived at Napoleon, presumably to pick up fuel, the townspeople pounced. With their cannons aimed at the steamer, soldiers swarmed aboard and took the vessel. Colonel W. Warren Johnson of the 6th Arkansas Infantry Regiment examined the ship and said that the *Belle* was "in good order, and well suited for the transportation of troops and supplies, having an excellent cabin, and the lower deck filled with bunks; she can transport comfortably 2000 troops. Her estimated value [is] $15,000." Denson wrote that the residents "had captured the Ohio Belle, taken her loading, and driven the passengers off without refunding any of their fare." He added that "the exciting news of the capture of the Ohio Belle spread like lightning up and down the river, and no boat would pass for several days, for fear of meeting the same fate." Although they missed some other Northern-owned vessels, Arkansas authorities had plans for the *Belle* to serve as a troop transport on the Mississippi River. The soldiers were also thrilled to capture the boat because fifteen hundred sacks of salt were on board, valued at $2,000. The rebels ignored Sebastian's cries of protest as they removed him and the crew and took control of the steamer. It would be years until Sebastian regained command of the boat.[6]

Northerners were furious that Arkansans had taken the vessel. Joseph Holt, an early Kentucky Unionist who became the Federal judge advocate general, wrote that the steamboat had been "seized by a band of rebel marauders at Napoleon, Ark." The *New York Tribune* complained that the *Belle* "was taken from her owners and the crew grossly insulted."[7]

Insulted, yes, but at least they were safe. Those aboard the *Westmoreland*, also taken at Napoleon, were not so fortunate. Like the *Belle*, the *Westmoreland* was traveling from New Orleans to Cincinnati. By the time the vessel stopped at Napoleon, the steamboat had a large number of passengers on board, including Southerners. A group of Napoleon residents boarded the *Westmoreland*, examined papers, and decided to allow the boat to continue northward. As the steamer prepared to leave the landing, however, more fervent citizens arrived and tied the boat to the shore. The captain of the boat shouted that he would "cut the lines and leave." In response, the citizens detaining the vessel said that they would fire upon the craft if it pulled away. The captain retorted that "they might fire and be d—d." He then cut the lines. As the boat backed from the landing, a newspaper reported, "the citizens attempted to fire a cannon which was within ten feet of her, but it flashed [misfired], and before the gun could be replaced, so as to strike the Westmoreland, she was out of reach, seeing which the citizens fired upon her with small arms, killing one man and injuring another." A horrified A. C. Denson wrote that "while the boat was backing out, the aforesaid infantry and belligerent citizens, poured an unceremonious broadside upon the unfortunate passengers, from their muskets and revolvers; repeating the same as fast as they could load." More than a dozen bullets ripped into the boat, peppering the siding, breaking windows, and striking Harry Hamner of Memphis, who was shot in the chest and killed. One of the crew, a fireman, was wounded in the shoulder. Thus, the Arkansans only killed a fellow Southerner.[8]

The *Westmoreland* rushed up the river. In order to avoid more trigger-happy secessionists, the boat bypassed Helena, Arkansas. This was a wise move, for when the *Mars* and *Hetty Gillmore* stopped there, residents claimed both of the Ohio-owned ships. When the *Westmoreland* reached Memphis, they offloaded Hamner's corpse. They were not, however, free from pro-Confederate residents. The mayor and other citizens boarded the vessel and searched the manifest. To prevent the *Westmoreland* from escaping, they stripped the cylinder heads from the engine and left a company of cadets on board to guard the ship. The *Westmoreland* was seized, they proclaimed, in retribution for Volunteer State weapons being detained on Northern soil. When the secessionists realized, however, that the boat "was partly owned in Kentucky" and was not solely operated by Cincinnati businessmen, the engine parts were returned and the vessel was allowed to continue its northward journey.[9]

Although Napoleon residents were gleeful with the capture of the *Belle,* the town eventually experienced the hard hand of war. By July 1862, the cost of the conflict was evident. "The 'City of Napoleon,'" one writer commented, "whose citizens were the first to fire into an unarmed boat, laden with scores of ladies and gentlemen, is the very picture of the 'deserted village.' The stores, hotels, and private dwellings were all closed, and not a white man was seen in the place." The writer only witnessed one enslaved man and a mule. For citizens of Napoleon, the palmy days of celebrating seized Yankee vessels were gone.[10]

Retribution continued as Unionist citizens captured Southern steamboats. Ships owned in seceded states were grabbed in Cincinnati. Residents in Madison, Indiana, snagged the Southern-owned *Lancaster No. 3.* In late April 1861, the *Louisville Daily Courier* observed that "the river trade is becoming more restricted every day, owing to the prevalence of mob law along the Northern line of the river, where ships of potatoes, fish, apples and other munitions of war are contraband, and of course are kept at home to rot."[11]

While the *Ohio Belle* remained tied to the Arkansas shore, the crew was fortunate to escape. Passengers and workers were allowed to leave Napoleon, and they boarded the *Kentucky* for the journey home. Although most of them were taken to Nashville, the officers of the *Belle* disembarked at St. Louis. Sebastian surely fumed during the entire journey. In fact, with his *Belle* in rebel hands, it galvanized him to act. He quickly joined the Union army, and it was said, "was among the first Ohio volunteers at the commencement of the war for gunboat service." Sebastian would serve his country on familiar waters and would take revenge on Confederates for the seizure of the *Ohio Belle.*[12]

By July 2, 1861, Sebastian was wearing Union blue as a pilot on the gunboat *Lexington.* His *Ohio Belle,* however, remained in rebel hands. Shortly after the Confederates captured the boat, rumors spread that they would use it and other vessels to attack Cairo, Illinois. Instead, the *Belle* and the *Mars* housed officers and sick soldiers. The *Belle* also served as a watchboat to scout for Federal vessels on the Mississippi River and to transport troops on the Mississippi and White Rivers. In mid-July 1861, for example, the *Belle* carried Colonel Patrick Cleburne's 1st Arkansas Infantry Regiment. In addition, Loreta Janeta Velazquez, a woman who claimed to have served the Confederacy disguised as Lieutenant "Harry T. Buford," said she once shipped her infantry battalion aboard the *Belle*. Although historian William C. Davis has debunked Velazquez's claims, calling her the most "ambitious female con artist of her time," it is telling that she included the *Ohio Belle* in her story.[13]

Confederate authorities frequently used the vessel as a hospital transport. In August 1861, assistant surgeon B. J. Dickinson published "a card" from aboard the *Belle*. "In [sic] behalf of the sick soldiers in my charge, from New Madrid," he wrote, "I would return our sincere thanks to Capt. Jerry Smith, for his kind and humane treatment during our passage from New Madrid, Mo., to Memphis, Tenn." Confederates also used the steamboat for transporting slaves. Brigadier General M. Jeff Thompson once requested that John J. Edson, then the captain of the *Belle*, move enslaved people from Missouri and Arkansas, "to the Tennessee side of the river." After the war, Edson continued to work in the packet steamboat business as captain of the *Gallatin*, which traveled across the river between Memphis and Arkansas.[14]

In some instances, Confederate officers treated the *Belle* as it was intended—a luxury mode of transport. In February 1862, General U. S. Grant sent a captain from the 33rd Illinois Infantry Regiment down the Mississippi River to deliver a letter pertaining to prisoner exchanges to Confederate authorities. The officer met the *Ohio Belle* on the Mississippi River near Columbus, Kentucky, under a "Confederate flag of truce." The officer stopped the *Belle* and went on board. He then handed Grant's letter to the commanding officer. "My proposition was curtly rejected," the officer wrote, "and my immediate departure suggested with some politeness and a good deal of earnestness. The 'Ohio Belle' was filled with officers and finely dressed ladies, who were evidently having a delightful time. The Confederacy was feeling a bit gayer just then than it did somewhat later." The Southern officers on board—who likely believed that the war would be over quickly—were celebrating and did not wish to be bothered with enemy correspondence and the details of prisoner exchange. The war could wait, for there was fun to be had on the luxurious *Ohio Belle*.[15]

Although Sebastian likely worried that the steamer would remain under Confederate control, the *Belle* was ultimately retrieved by Union soldiers tasked with opening the Mississippi River. In order to block that river, Southern forces constructed artillery emplacements at Island No. 10, a mile-long island near New Madrid, Missouri. In March 1862, a Northern flotilla descended onto the island to bombard it into submission. When the Union ships approached, the *Belle* appeared at a bend in the river to reconnoiter the Federal vessels. The *Benton,* a Union ship, fired on the *Belle* and drove off the steamboat. One reporter accompanying the flotilla wrote that "a steamer was seen coming up the river from the island. Near and nearer she approaches us, until we can read her name, Ohio Belle, painted in large letters upon her wheel-house. The saucy craft continues her course and rounds the point in full view of our whole fleet. The Benton fires at her, and she instantly puts about and goes down the river like a scared deer, nor ever stops until her smoke pipes are lost to view among the heavy timber upon the head of the island." Another witness said that the *Ohio Belle* and several other boats were "steaming up and down with that perplexity which you sometimes see in an ant hill, a hornet's nest or among wasps when disturbed or hemmed in. They move up and down seemingly with no object in view." Helpless to defend the island from the Union fleet, the *Belle* steamed away. The Federal boats then moved forward and bombarded Island No. 10.[16]

When the Confederates realized that surrender was imminent, they decided to destroy the *Belle* to keep it out of Union hands. The rebels knocked holes in the hull and set it adrift down the river. Although they hoped that the *Belle* would sink quickly, one witness said that a Union transport spotted the boat and towed it to New Madrid. There, "steam pumps were rigged, the holes in her hull stopped, and she is now all right, ready to do

When the *Ohio Belle* was under Confederate control, the Union gunboat *Benton* fired at the vessel near Island No. 10 and drove off the steamboat. (Public Library of Cincinnati and Hamilton County)

yeoman service for the Union." The *Belle,* then valued at $25,000 and called "a fine Cincinnati built steamer," had been saved.[17]

After the war, a former Union soldier looking for a salvage bounty told a different story. When Island No. 10 fell, the Confederates scuttled the boat and set it adrift. When the boat neared the shore near New Madrid, Union soldiers, including the "old and experienced steamboat man" Sergeant David Armstrong, pulled the *Belle* in. Armstrong, also called "an old river man," went aboard. He crept into the hold, where he waded through neck-deep water to patch the hole that the rebels had bashed into the *Belle.* Armstrong plugged the damage and saved the steamer from sinking. He certainly put his life on the line; according to his claim, while in the neck-deep water, "if the boat had rolled or pitched over he would have lost his life." Armstrong noted that the steamboat "was a boat about 700 tons burden, and was worth about $40,000." Although Armstrong had hoped for a salvage bounty, he was not paid. Because he took the risk while he was in the Federal service, it was considered all in a day's work for "an old and experienced steamboat man" serving in the Union army.[18]

Once the *Ohio Belle* was repaired, Northern soldiers put the eight-year-old steamer to good use. Although the boat's owners "repeatedly demanded" that it be returned, the *Belle* instead took an active part in Union operations on the Mississippi River. Shortly after being placed under Federal service, the *Ohio Belle* delivered Confederate prisoners of war from Island No. 10 to Cairo. It also served as a transport for Union soldiers.[19]

Running steamboats along shorelines in Confederate territory was dangerous work. Federal gunboats frequently traveled with the *Belle* and other Union vessels. This was done, one soldier noted, to protect them from "the guerrillas that infested the river." Accidents also posed a danger. In one instance, Private Henry M. Eddy of Company B, 58th Illinois Infantry Regiment fell off the *John H. Groesbeck* while carrying "a bundle of clothing down into the cabin." He died, a soldier wrote, "although he struggled desperately to save himself from a watery grave." Furthermore, an hour before Eddy's death, guerrillas on the Arkansas side of the river fired at the boat and killed four Union soldiers who were on board.[20]

Disease and illness were a constant threat to soldiers during the Civil War, and troops on the *Ohio Belle* also succumbed to sickness. On February 6, 1863, twenty-three-year-old Samuel Nelson of the 31st Iowa Infantry Regiment died on board the *Belle* at Young's Point, Louisiana. Four days later, Corporal Henry Barnes of the 96th Ohio Infantry Regiment died at St. Louis after being left sick on the *Belle*. That August, nineteen-year-old Eli E. Vail of the 19th Iowa Infantry Regiment died on board near Natchez, Mississippi. The soldiers also faced accidents. Private Henry Robinson of the 13th Connecticut Infantry Regiment, for example, "was lost overboard and drowned at night." Many of the troops who passed away on steamboats were simply buried in the river. One who died from an illness on the *Omaha*, a soldier wrote, "was put in a coffin and consigned to the deep, to know the turmoils of earth no more." He added, "We know not who was left to mourn at home, or whether friends ever knew of his fate."[21]

In April 1862, the *Ohio Belle, Sam Getty, Spread Eagle,* and *McDowell* transported the 8th Wisconsin Infantry Regiment on the Mississippi River. One member of that unit described the journey on what may have been the *Belle*. "This evening we are in the elegant cabin of our steamer," he wrote.

> It is a long spacious cabin, decorated in elegant style with large mirrors, costly furniture, and occupied by as merry a crowd as ever assembled on the Mississippi. The chandeliers are brilliantly lighted up and the evening's entertainment has begun. In one end of the cabin, seated around a table are our staff officers, with several good looking ladies, playing whist, at another table are some ten or fifteen officers enjoying a simple game of euchre. At another table near the centre [*sic*] of the room, some half a dozen . . . are writing letters. Some are singing, others telling snake stories and *all* are smoking.[22]

Although the luxurious surroundings helped the soldiers forget the war, service on the *Belle* was not always filled with ladies, card games, and cigar smoke. On one voyage, the steamboat took troops on a mission of retribution. In September 1862, after Confederate guerrillas fired on the US supply ship *Eugene* from Randolph, Tennessee, Union General William T. Sherman ordered Federal soldiers to burn Randolph as punishment for harboring guerrillas. The *Belle* transported an Ohio infantry regiment and an artillery battery to the town. As the steamboat neared the shore, one Buckeye wrote, "the quiet citizens . . . began to scamper like rats from a foundering vessel. Oh, but they did run." He added that "the whole town felt their impending doom, and were satisfied that it was just, altho' hard." The Union troops laid the town to waste, burning all buildings except for the Methodist church. Approximately sixty houses were put to the torch. One of the Ohioans wrote that this was done "to measure out exemplary and speedy chastisement." The citizens, the soldier added, were allowed "to move all their household furniture from their dwellings" as he took "horses, mules, negroes and cotton found in the place. After which I proceeded to apply the desolating torch to every building in town but the church, which we left standing to mark the spot where once stood the town of Randolph."[23]

About a month later, the *Belle* took Union soldiers to burn a plantation in Arkansas. This journey, however, was interrupted

During the Civil War, John Sebastian, captain of the *Ohio Belle*, lost his arm while piloting the Union gunboat *A. O. Tyler*. A "timberclad" gunboat, white oak planks protected the crew and the vessel.

when the steamer "unshipped her rudder and was decidedly in improper condition for the voyage." The Yankee torchbearers were instead transported on the *Catahoula*. The *Belle* was soon repaired; in November 1862, the steamer joined a fleet that took sixteen thousand Union troops to attack Helena, Arkansas. A month later, the vessel transported more Federal artillery, cavalry, and infantry on the Mississippi River and up the Yazoo River.[24]

While the *Ohio Belle* was carrying Northern troops, John Sebastian was a pilot on the Union gunboat *A. O. Tyler*. Just like the *Belle*, the *Tyler* was a packet boat that, before the war, had run the Ohio and Mississippi Rivers. A 575-ton, side-wheel steamboat with a six-foot draft and named for its original owner, the US War Department purchased the vessel in Cincinnati in mid-1861 for $20,666. The four-year-old boat was initially outfitted with one 12-pounder smoothbore howitzer, one 32-pounder, and six 8-inch guns. It was also reinforced with white oak planks to protect the nearly seventy-man crew from fire. These armaments made the *Tyler* a formidable timber-clad gunboat.[25]

The *Tyler,* which frequently worked alongside the gunboat *Lexington,* had an active career on the Mississippi and Yazoo Rivers. In September 1861, the *Tyler* skirmished with a Confederate gunboat near Hickman. A month later, the vessel was scouting for enemy troops near Columbus, Kentucky, which was then controlled by Southern forces. Rebel artillery shells nearly struck the boat, so the *Tyler* fired on an enemy camp before scooting back upriver.[26]

In November, Union General U. S. Grant's army landed near Belmont, Missouri, across the river from Columbus, where they defeated Southern troops. Grant noted that the *Tyler* "rendered most efficient service" by shelling Confederate artillery batteries at Columbus while protecting Union transport vessels. The *Tyler* was not immune to casualties. At least one crew member was decapitated and two men were wounded when a rebel artillery shell struck the boat.[27]

In early 1862 the *Tyler* participated in the capture of Fort Henry on the Tennessee River and Fort Donelson on the Cumberland River before moving up the Tennessee River to support a Union assault on Florence, Alabama. The *Tyler* and other Federal vessels destroyed bridges and enemy supplies, and captured the steamboat *Alfred Robb.* In another incident, the *Tyler* raided around Eastport, Mississippi. There, the crew confiscated Confederate wheat and flour.[28]

In early April 1862, Confederate forces led by General Albert Sidney Johnston moved against General U. S. Grant's army at Pittsburg Landing, Tennessee. On April 6, Johnston's troops surprised Grant's force in a blistering attack that sent the Union troops reeling back to the Tennessee River. As the Confederate army advanced, the *Tyler* and the *Lexington* helped repulse the rebels. The two boats then took turns shelling Confederate troops throughout the night. Union reinforcements arrived, Grant staged a counterattack the next morning, and the Federal troops emerged victorious in what became known as the Battle of Shiloh. Because of the *Tyler's* role in helping blunt the Southern assault, the US secretary of the navy gave the vessel a letter of commendation.[29]

In July 1862, Union authorities learned that the Confederate ironclad gunboat *Arkansas* was operating up the Yazoo River. A new vessel armed with ten guns, manned by more than 230 men, and protected by armored plating, the *Arkansas* was intent on protecting Vicksburg, Mississippi. In order to secure control of the water around Vicksburg, the *Tyler*, along with the ironclad gunboat *Carondelet*, and the *Queen of the West*, a packet boat converted into a ram, moved up the Yazoo River to scout for the enemy ship. At six o'clock in the morning on July 15, the three Union boats encountered the *Arkansas* as it moved downstream. Sebastian was piloting the *Tyler* as the *Arkansas* appeared.[30]

The *Tyler* fired on the *Arkansas*, but it was soon evident that the three Union ships were no match for the armored rebel vessel. Firing, the boats turned away from the *Arkansas* and moved to escape downriver. The Confederate ironclad immediately engaged the *Carondelet* and peppered the Federal boat with shot. The crew recorded that "our wheel ropes were shot away, steam escape pipe cut, exhaust pipe cut, cold water supply pipe riddled with pieces of shot, and steam gauge shot away, the boat becoming unmanageable." Out of control, the *Carondelet* ran up on a stump, got snagged, and fired on the *Arkansas* as the rebel boat passed by, following the *Tyler* down the river.[31]

The *Arkansas* was dogged in its pursuit. After the *Carondelet* ran aground, the crew of the *Queen of the West* had seen enough. An officer on the *Tyler* wrote that the *Queen* "behaved in the most cowardly and dastardly manner, basely deserting us without making an attempt to bring his vessel in action." With the *Queen* steaming off, the *Arkansas* turned its attention to the *Tyler*. In the ensuing fight, the *Tyler* had eight killed and eighteen wounded, including Sebastian, who lost his left arm. Lieutenant William Gwin, who commanded the Union boat, noted that "Pilots Sebastian and Hiner displayed their usual coolness in handling the vessel under the very trying circumstances, and I think deserve the greatest praise. [Sebastian] did not leave the wheel until he lost his arm."[32]

Despite the casualties, the *Tyler* meted out vengeance on the enemy crew. According to Isaac Brown, the captain of the rebel vessel, a shot from the *Tyler* cut through the pilothouse and lopped

While fighting the Confederate vessel *Arkansas*, the crew of the *A. O. Tyler* sustained eight men killed and eighteen wounded. This included John Sebastian, who lost his left arm. (Public Library of Cincinnati and Hamilton County)

off part of the wheel. The shot also killed one pilot and wounded another. Moreover, when the *Arkansas* neared the *Tyler*, soldiers on the Union boat unleashed a volley of musketry. Although most of the rounds bounced harmlessly off of the *Arkansas's* iron shell, one bullet shot through a porthole and struck Brown in the temple, leaving the rebel captain alive but stunned. Despite this damage, the *Arkansas* bested the *Tyler* in the fray, leaving many men killed and Sebastian permanently disabled.[33]

The *Queen of the West* and the damaged *Tyler* limped back to the Union fleet that consisted of twenty-two boats waiting in the Mississippi River at the mouth of the Yazoo River. Facing overwhelming odds, the *Arkansas* made a break for it. The ironclad steamed through the Union fleet, weapons blazing, hell-bent on reaching the safety of friendly artillery batteries at Vicksburg. "The ram *Queen of the West* soon came in sight with a full head of steam on and making for the flagship, followed by the *Tyler*, firing her stern guns rapidly at the approaching ram and gun-boat *Arkansas*," a Union sailor wrote. The Union boats unleashed a barrage at the *Arkansas*, but the rebel ironclad passed by the Federal vessels, "keeping up a constant firing as she went, and receiving our shots without any apparent damage to her." Much to the embarrassment of the Union fleet, the *Arkansas* safely made it to Vicksburg.[34]

The fate of one Union boat illustrates how Federal vessels suffered from the *Arkansas's* fire. A shell from the Confederate craft punctured the *Lancaster's* steam drum, scalding several crew members, including the head engineer and the second engineer, who jumped overboard before being "shot in the water." The assistant engineer was killed, a cook was scalded and died, and a deckhand had "both legs and one arm shot off and badly scalded, [and] died in a few minutes." Several others were killed and wounded, including the pilot, who "stuck to the wheel till he dropped from the platform . . . scalded inwardly, wounded in the left side, right shoulder broken, and teeth all blown out." The *Lancaster* was disabled, "having been shot all to pieces." The crew of the boat consisted of 169 men, which included forty-three African Americans. At the end of the fight, only six of the black crew members remained unscathed.[35]

Sebastian's wound disabled him for further military service. Therefore, he returned to Cincinnati, where he lived at 416 West 9th Street. Although Sebastian was no longer in uniform, he helped the Union war effort by spearheading naval recruiting in the Queen City. In February 1863, for example, he took fifty recruits to Cairo, Illinois, "for the naval depot at that point." During this time the *Ohio Belle* continued to operate under Federal service and was part of a fleet that transported Union troops down the Mississippi River. The *Belle* and the other boats passed Napoleon, Arkansas, where the *Belle* had fallen into rebel hands. One soldier on the *Omaha* wrote that Napoleon was "once a thrifty place, but now deserted; only a few forlorn looking women and children could be seen. 'Twas a true picture of a deserted village. Oh! the horrors of war."[36]

In June 1863, the *Belle* transported both Union soldiers and

During the secession crisis, citizens of Madison, Indiana, seized the Southern-owned *Lancaster No. 3*. Converted into a Union gunboat, the crew of the vessel suffered horrific casualties after it was "shot all to pieces" by the Confederate ironclad *Arkansas*. (Public Library of Cincinnati and Hamilton County)

Confederate prisoners of war who had been captured during the Vicksburg campaign. Two months later, while the steamer operated north of Vicksburg, one soldier commented that the crew left much to be desired. "We have a very poor pilot," he wrote. "He has run us on sand bars 4 times." Historian Earl J. Hess writes that the pilot struck one sandbar so hard "that the deck wrenched six inches forward of the hull and the engine stopped." Sebastian, sitting at home, would have been enraged at the treatment of his *Ohio Belle*.[37]

In September 1863, while the *Belle* hauled ammunition and ordnance to Union troops, Federal military authorities took stock of the vessels they were using on the Mississippi River. They determined that the *Belle* could haul seven hundred troops, 175 animals, and fifteen wagons. This assessment categorized the *Belle* as a smaller vessel; the larger steamers *Luminary, J. C. Swan,* and the *Ed. Walsh,* for example, could each transport one thousand troops, 250 animals, and thirty wagons.[38]

Smaller vessels like the *Belle* were evidently no longer needed for the Northern war effort. A month later, the Union military returned the *Belle* to its owners, who eventually received $19,145 for the boat's use in Federal service. Sebastian, despite his lost arm, again became master of the vessel and immediately returned to running trade from Cincinnati to New Orleans, which by May 1862 had fallen under Union control. Although the *Belle* was again delivering freight along the Ohio and Mississippi Rivers, the boat still occasionally transported Union troops.[39]

As the *Belle* again took civilian cargo southward, the crew was frequently reminded that they were steaming through a war zone. In March 1864, a seventy-year-old man who lived on the Tennessee side of the Mississippi River near New Madrid boarded the boat. The man said that he and three neighbors were chopping wood when guerrillas appeared and killed his companions. They called the survivor a "d——d old abolitionist" and told him to run. As he made for the woods, the guerrillas shot him in the arm and hand. For several days the wounded man crawled to safety until he was finally seen by the crew of the *Belle.* Captain Sebastian "treated him generously," and a military surgeon on the boat "dressed his wounds."[40]

Transporting troops also kept the war foremost in the minds of Sebastian and his crew. In April 1864 as part of the Red River campaign, the *Ohio Belle* carried soldiers and supplies. During that excursion, two soldiers were severely injured when guerrillas fired on the vessel. After the battles of Mansfield and Pleasant Hill, Louisiana, the *Belle* took wounded Union soldiers to New Orleans. This included a run on April 16, when the boat transported more than three hundred injured and nearly sixty prisoners of war. The *Belle* continued to carry troops for several more months. In September 1864, Colonel L. A. Sheldon used the steamboat as his headquarters while it sat off of the Louisiana coast.[41]

As the Civil War ended, the *Ohio Belle* continued to assist Federal operations. In April 1865, as General Robert E. Lee's Army of Northern Virginia surrendered at Appomattox Courthouse, the *Belle* was working as a "flag-of-truce boat," carrying fifty bales of cotton that were to be sold to benefit prisoners of war and the people of Louisiana. Two months later, Union Brigadier General R. A. Cameron requested that the *Belle* be used to keep lines of communication open between Union armies.[42]

By this time, however, Sebastian no longer commanded the *Ohio Belle*. Instead, he was master of the *John H. Groesbeck*, a boat called a "superb steamer" that also ran the Cincinnati to New Orleans trade route and had transported soldiers during the war. It appears that, by the end of the conflict, the *Belle* had been sold to the Federal government, which pushed Sebastian out of work on the *Belle* and forced him to find a new steamboat to manage.[43]

8

A High Sense of Truth and Honor

Those who were aboard the *Ohio Belle* in 1856 during the murder of Hiram Stevens eventually disembarked and returned to their work, families, and lives. Matilda Heron, the actress who was suspected of releasing the murderer "Jones," continued to play the role of Camille to much acclaim in cities up and down the Ohio and Mississippi Rivers. On March 24, 1856, shortly after leaving the *Belle*, she performed *Camille* at the Gaiety Theatre in New Orleans. Crowds and critics alike were thrilled at the "new scenery, properties, and decorations" that enlivened the play. For the rest of the year she toured the nation, performing in New York and other cities. In March 1857, she took her powerful, emotive acting to the role of Medea, which was favorably compared to her performances in *Camille*. Although Heron developed health problems during the 1860s, not even the Civil War stopped her art. In 1862, she performed *Camille* in Indianapolis. Six years later, she left the grind of the road to teach acting. She died on March 7, 1877, after an operation. She was only forty-six years old.[1]

Joseph Cocke Sr. of Holly Springs, Mississippi, the father of the man who killed Stevens, continued his work in farming, business, and politics. After the Civil War, Cocke was an officer of the Holly Springs Savings and Insurance Company and the Bank of Holly Springs. Despite his son having murdered the clerk on the *Ohio Belle*, Cocke remained a prominent resident of Holly Springs. In 1874, he broke his leg in a train wreck. In reporting the accident, the *Memphis Daily Appeal*, which continued to prop up the reputation of the Cocke family, called Cocke "an old and respected citizen of this place." On his death in November 1884, the newspaper repeated the assessment. "Capt. Joseph Cock, an old and respected citizen," they wrote, "died in his home in this city on the 18th instant, in the eighty-seventh year of his age. Capt. Cock was a man of great force of character, of unbending integrity, tenaciousness of purpose and was always actuated by a high sense of truth and honor." The same, however, could not be said of his departed son.[2]

Captain John Sebastian remained on the rivers for a few more years after the Civil War, serving as master of the *Groesbeck*. He worked this "large and superb side-wheel passenger steamer," throughout 1866. That year, his wife, called "a most noble woman," passed away. "This cast a deep gloom over his life," his obituary stated. Sebastian left the steamboat trade and "remained at home" in Cincinnati, where he lived at 368 West 9th Street. A year later, he suffered from a "dangerous illness" and was thought to be near death. He recovered, however, and the *Evansville Daily Journal* wrote, "We hope soon to find the Captain around among his many friends."[3]

In 1867, those friends pushed Sebastian to run for the office of Hamilton County (Cincinnati) treasurer, which was called "one of the most lucrative and responsible offices in Ohio." He ran as a Union Party candidate, and, a newspaper contended, "Owing to the large majority of the party, the nomination is equivalent to an election." He won the nomination before securing the general election by a 1,792 vote majority. He served for two years. The salary of the position was an estimated $30,000, a sizeable sum for the late 1860s.[4]

When Sebastian's term as county treasurer ended, he moved to Emporia, Kansas, with his family. There, he became successful raising cattle. In 1875, at age fifty-eight, he lived with his extended family and owned $16,000 in real estate and $25,000 in personal property. Sebastian also invested in railroads and land. He supposedly named the town of Newton, Kansas, after the Santa Fe Railroad expanded there from Emporia "to catch the Texas cattle trade."[5]

This one-armed Union veteran was recognized for being level-headed in times of crisis. In March 1872, there was a large fire in Emporia that burned a number of buildings and threatened the rest of the town. Sebastian and another man stood guard at a friend's general store and waited for the blaze to move in that direction. If flames reached the building, the two men were prepared to move the store's goods before the fire consumed the structure. "They are cool headed gentlemen," the *Emporia News* reported, "and kept the doors closed."[6]

In October 1875, Sebastian became "dangerously ill from softening of the brain," a nineteenth-century term used to describe dementia. A doctor from Cincinnati traveled to Emporia to try to help. The illness became more severe, and Sebastian was "attacked with aphelxia, which involved the loss of memory." From that point forward, Sebastian needed constant care. Despite around-the-clock nursing, "incurable sores ensued, and for some months he . . . rapidly declined."[7]

Sebastian died of "brain congestion" (likely a stroke) at his home on Merchant's Street in Emporia on July 11, 1876. On his death, his obituary stated, "He was a man of strong will and constitution, and his nature yielded slowly." It added that "the deep sorrow of the family at his death was shared by all who knew him." Another obituary said that "he was a man much esteemed by all." Sebastian's funeral was held at his home. His body was then taken to the Santa Fe depot and shipped to Cincinnati. He was buried next to his wife in Spring Grove Cemetery there, where his former clerk, the murdered Hiram Stevens, also lies buried.[8]

The ultimate fate of the *Ohio Belle* mirrored that of the entire steamboat industry. After the Civil War, the use of steamboats continued to decline as railroad lines expanded. This was a death knell for the *Belle,* which, by the end of the conflict, was an aged vessel. Furthermore, because the boat spent the war years as a soldiers' transport that also carried sick and wounded men, the boat was surely in rough shape. The *Ohio Belle* was no longer in the luxurious condition of its former, pre-war self.[9]

In the late summer of 1865, an advertisement appeared in newspapers noting a "large government sale" of "Steamboats,

Wharf-Boats, Barges, and other Property." Dozens of Federal vessels used during the Civil War were to be sold at New Orleans, including the "side-wheel steamer Ohio Belle, registered 300 tons." The Quartermaster General's Department in Washington, DC, took sealed bids for the sale through October 4, 1865. Three months later, the *Ohio Belle* sold at New Orleans "to parties in Alabama" for $6,250, a far cry from her estimated value of $20,000 from just a year earlier.[10]

The steamboat's name would not survive the sale. On being sold, the boat was renamed the *Alabama Belle*. This was actually a shrewd business move. In the Deep South immediately after the Civil War, a steamer imbued with a Yankee state's name would probably not have done good business. Therefore, the *Ohio Belle* transformed into the *Alabama Belle*. It then traveled the Alabama River, transporting goods and people to Mobile, Montgomery, and other landings. W. C. Wagley served as the master, and Burr Brent was the clerk. If John Sebastian was following the sale, the one-armed Union veteran surely bristled when the *Belle* was renamed to honor a southern state.[11]

In September 1866, the *Belle* was sold again. The *New Orleans Times-Picayune* ran a notice stating that "capitalists and steam boatmen should take note," because an auction house was selling the "fine steamboat Alabama Belle, with all her tackle, apparel and furniture, in complete order, as she now lies at the foot of Napoleon Avenue. As a safe and profitable investment she will no doubt prove invaluable, and the sale should be well attended."[12]

Sadly, the *Belle* did not survive long after the auction. In 1867, after a miraculous twelve-year run on multiple rivers, the steamboat was "broken up" and likely sold for scrap. As her boilers and boards were taken away and windows and wheels dismantled, one wonders if those pulling her apart knew her history and the tales of murder and desperate men who once rode over dark waters on the grand *Ohio Belle*.[13]

Conclusion

When Alexis de Tocqueville visited Cincinnati, the home of the *Ohio Belle,* he wrote that "all that there is of good or bad in American society is to be found there." Although the French political scientist was describing the city, he could have been referring to the vessel itself. All classes of society—including gentlemen, merchants, actresses, soldiers, gamblers, thieves, and murderers—came together on the *Ohio Belle.* Because these passengers hailed from a broad cross section of the nation, as the straw poll taken on the vessel during the election of President William Henry Harrison attests, interactions on board the small space of a steamboat highlighted regional differences and revealed multiple tensions found within antebellum society.

Those regional peculiarities could cause friction. On the *Ohio Belle,* Stevens's murder and his killer's subsequent execution detail the strain that existed between those who followed the code of honor and those who did not. Although most Americans, as historian Lorien Foote explains, followed some sort of code during the nineteenth century, upper class, white southern males viewed honor as a dispassionate compass that guided their daily lives. It also set them apart from the common fray. If, for example, they were insulted by a member of the lower class, the code called for an immediate response. Therefore, when Stevens questioned Cocke about his counterfeit money, it meant that the menial clerk was calling him—a planter's son—a liar. Furthermore, when Stevens pushed Cocke out of the cabin, Stevens denigrated the Mississippian's manhood. Within the strictures of Cocke's code, and because he was part of that "touch wood gentry," Cocke immediately responded with violence. Only this, in his mind, would remove the stain on his honor. Once the crew caught him on deck, Cocke sought to reinforce his honor by stating that he would face trial, even if he might hang for the crime. In Cocke's world, bravely facing death was another way to claim status. The killer, however, never had that chance, for angry crew members placed vengeance for their dead friend above Cocke's claims of honor.

In addition to Stevens's murder, the history of the *Ohio Belle* illustrates how Americans contended with violence along western rivers during the mid-nineteenth century. Passengers and crew witnessed brutality in multiple forms: homicide, slavery, steamboat accidents, warfare, and more. They also perpetrated violence when they lashed Cocke to a chair and drowned him. Their turn to vigilantism is, however, unsurprising, considering that western river towns carried out mob-driven reprisals before Stevens's murder. In Louisville, xenophobic, native-born Americans murdered Irish and German immigrants during the "Bloody Monday" riots. Residents of that city also lynched the enslaved men acquitted of murdering the Joyce family. They also burned jurors and lawyers in effigy once Matt Ward was freed after killing his brother's teacher. Therefore, when authorities at Cairo balked at prosecuting Cocke, they allowed those on the *Ohio Belle* to become his judge, jury, and executioner.

In addition to the vigilantism perpetrated on Cocke and the various riots in Louisville, the story of the *Ohio Belle* demonstrates how nineteenth-century Americans embraced retribution. During the secession crisis, Southerners sought payback on Northern vessels when cities above the Mason-Dixon Line seized cargo bound for the Confederacy. This included the *Ohio Belle* and the *Westmoreland*, which met the wrath—and gunfire—of the citizens of Napoleon, Arkansas. In addition, once the *Ohio Belle* fell into rebel hands, the boat's captain, John Sebastian, joined the Union military so that he could exact vengeance upon Southern vessels. Wartime retribution involving the *Ohio Belle* continued after Union troops recaptured the boat. To avenge guerrilla depredations, they transported soldiers on the steamer to burn Randolph,

Tennessee. After the war, perhaps the *Ohio Belle* should have been renamed *Retaliation;* regardless, the boat's history and the riots that influenced its crew and passengers demonstrate how antebellum society embraced vengeance.

The murder on the *Ohio Belle* also illustrates how wealth and class prejudice influenced media coverage. After the public learned Cocke's true identity, Memphis newspapers, located near the murderer's hometown of Holly Springs, Mississippi, downplayed the killer's violent past and shifted blame for Stevens's murder onto the victim. The clerk, they argued, as they tried to impress Cocke's wealthy surviving family members, should not have questioned a "man of property." Most important, Stevens should not have used physical force against a member of the planter elite. Whereas the crew should have been condemned for drowning Cocke, the resulting class prejudice unfairly impugned the victim.

On March 7, 1856, a week before the *Ohio Belle* picked up "J. B. Jones" at Smithland, Kentucky, the abolitionist newspaper *The Liberator* published an article titled "Underground Railroad." This piece noted multiple instances in which enslaved people escaped Kentucky by crossing the icy Ohio River. In addition to mentioning fourteen slaves who passed to "the other side of Jordan," the article noted that "four more of the slaves of Mr. Gaines, the owner of Margaret Garner, have made successful flight, while he has been attending the trial of the fugitives" in Cincinnati.[1] Anyone familiar with western rivers, including readers of *The Liberator* and passengers on the *Ohio Belle,* knew the economic and political complexities of traveling the borderland between freedom and slavery.

The *Ohio Belle* reinforced the peculiar institution by transporting enslaved people like Samuel Watson along that borderland. As a northern-owned vessel that carried human cargo, the *Belle* profited from, and supported, the institution of slavery, further illustrating the tensions of the river border. In doing so, the *Belle* ran the risk of becoming mired in political consequences, including fugitive slave cases. This happened when Watson wandered off the *Belle* at Cincinnati, and Henry Hoppess had authorities declare him to be a fugitive slave. Although the crew of the *Belle* did not stick around to watch the court proceedings—there was, of course, a profit to be made—the Hoppess-Watson case reinforced fugitive slave laws by determining that slaves on boats tied to free soil were not themselves free. They were instead fugitive slaves, even if they were mere inches from the free shore. For enslaved African Americans, court cases like this meant that the "other side of Jordan" became a bit farther away.

It was, as the story of the *Ohio Belle* details, the fluidity of the border region and the strength of fugitive slave laws that enabled escaped slaves like Margaret Garner to cross the Ohio River to freedom. This fluidity also allowed them to be quickly returned to bondage. This was true even if an escaped enslaved person, like Garner, committed homicide. It is unsurprising that Garner's owner chose steamboat travel as the best way to carry his human chattel into the Deep South. This mode of transport meant that Garner could speedily escape the murder indictment in Ohio after she killed her daughter. Her owner cared nothing about justice in that case; instead, he was only concerned about keeping his property—a flight risk—under control. After the wreck of the *Henry Lewis*, which occurred shortly before Cocke killed Stevens on the *Ohio Belle*, Garner possibly sought to seize some control over her life in the chaos of that accident by allowing her infant to drown. As Garner and Watson discovered, perhaps those borders were not so fluid after all.

The Civil War, of course, ultimately shattered that border. By viewing that conflict through the lens of the *Ohio Belle*, we better understand how Northern-owned vessels, and their passengers and crew, fared on Southern waters during the secession crisis and the war. In addition to being caught in a cycle of retribution as Dixieland communities seized Yankee boats, the *Ohio Belle's* wartime participation as a hospital ship and military transport meant that an unknown number of soldiers died on board from wounds or illness. Travelers on the *Belle* also witnessed guerrilla depredations and the horrors of war as plantations and even whole communities were put to the torch.

The crew of the *Belle* was not immune to wartime suffering.

After the rebels captured the vessel, the boat's captain, John Sebastian, lost his arm while piloting a Union gunboat. Sebastian survived this grievous wound and was ultimately able to reclaim the boat and return it to the rivers. The war, however, had taken its toll. In addition to having lost his arm, Sebastian spent the rest of his life shrouded by a restless spirit, especially after the death of his wife. The *Ohio Belle* also suffered from the war; abused by military service, it paled in comparison to its former glory. The boat was eventually sold and scrapped.

By the time the *Ohio Belle* was pulled apart, Joseph Cocke and Hiram Stevens had been dead and buried for more than a decade. Their final resting places exemplify how each man should be remembered.

When Cocke went on the run after killing his friend in Holly Springs, Mississippi, he assumed the false name of "J. B. Jones." Few would have considered him to be an honorable man. After his death, however, the press near his hometown propped up his fallen reputation. In their view, the insulted and misunderstood Mississippian rightfully responded to Stevens with immediate violence when the clerk insulted him. Although many southerners would have nodded with approval had Cocke caned or horsewhipped the Cincinnati clerk, shooting the unarmed man in a fit of drunken passion was outright murder. As southern newspapers spun the tale, however, they explained that a "man of property" would not have murdered a lower-class clerk without provocation. Therefore, Stevens's death was his own fault, and postmortem honor was conferred on Cocke because he came from a wealthy family.

Although Cocke's honor code pushed him to murder Stevens, the Mississippian was not ultimately an honorable man. Arrogant, impetuous, and petulant, he could not control his passion, as both of his murders attest. Furthermore, his drunkenness and dissipation, coupled with the lies that he spun while traveling under an assumed name, including the use of counterfeit money, proved that he was no gentleman. Yet, he did retain the touchiness of a member of the southern gentry, and it was that culturally reinforced character flaw, stoked by alcohol and class prejudice, that led him to kill Stevens. The crew and passengers, who bound him to a chair and threw him into the churning river, never considered Cocke's social status. Knowing that authorities were loath to prosecute the Mississippian, they followed other communities along the Ohio River—and their own riverine code as it pertained to criminals on board their vessel—and took the law into their own hands.

Today, Cocke's final resting place is unknown. His father retrieved his remains, so it is probable that he was buried in the Cocke family plot in Holly Springs, Mississippi. Because he now lies buried in an unmarked grave, his family likely believed that he had lost his honor and disgraced the family. By failing to mark his final resting place, they essentially erased the killer from their family record. At least those who wish to pay their respects to the murdered Stevens can visit his grave in Cincinnati and remember him. For a southern culture that valued ancestry and remembrance, having no visible grave means that Cocke's spirit, for all intents and purposes, still remains submerged under the churning western waters, forever linked to the *Ohio Belle.*

Acknowledgments

Multiple people assisted with this project, including Nathan Lynn of the McCracken County Public Library, who provided information about "roustabout" songs. Bobby Mitchell and Jim Moore of the Marshall County Historical Museum in Holly Springs, Mississippi, helped with information about the Cocke family and their burial site. Historian James M. Prichard provided suggestions for images, and offered kind words of encouragement. Albert Hallenberg and Jim Mainger, both with the Public Library of Cincinnati and Hamilton County, Ohio, and Jeff Dycus and Cheri Daniels of the Kentucky Historical Society, helped procure images. Friends Don Rightmyer, Bonnie Rightmyer, and Tim Talbott read the manuscript and offered valuable suggestions, as did my parents, Dr. Taylor Sanders, a retired history professor, and Barbara W. Sanders, a former English teacher. Colleagues Greg Hardison and Keith Jackson offered continual encouragement. Dr. Patrick Lewis provided helpful insight for the book's introduction. I am grateful to all of these kind people for their support.

I also thank the anonymous readers from the University Press of Kentucky for providing structural and interpretive advice. They have helped make this a better book. I also thank the board of directors and the staff of the University Press of Kentucky, notably acquisitions editor Patrick O'Dowd and publicity manager Mack McCormick, for their support of this project.

Finally, and most important, I thank my wonderful wife, Jenny, and my children, John, Anne, and Elizabeth, for their love and for pulling me off board the *Ohio Belle* when it was needed.

Acknowledgments

I have been fortunate to work in the public history field for more than two decades. That journey began as a teenage docent at the Lee Chapel in my hometown of Lexington, Virginia. The man who hired me there was the late Captain Robert C. Peniston. Before his job running the museum, Captain Peniston had a stellar career in the US Navy, which included serving as captain of the *USS New Jersey*. Although Captain Peniston never guided a nineteenth-century steamboat down the Ohio and Mississippi Rivers, he did serve as a navigator on President Harry S. Truman's presidential yacht. Because of Captain Peniston's naval career, friendship, and his love of history, I hope that he would have enjoyed this book. I know that he would have encouraged me to write it. Therefore, I dedicate this book to him, my late friend and first mentor in the museum and public history field.

Notes

Introduction

1. "A Shocking Scene in the West," *Shepherdstown Register*, April 5, 1856.

2. Hardin used the term in an 1838 murder case. Lucius P. Little, *Ben Hardin, His Times and Contemporaries* (Louisville: Courier-Journal Job Printing, 1887), 307; "Human Life" from "Harrodsburg," *Louisville Courier-Journal*, January 5, 1874. A few days later, the journalist added, "While men are walking magazines, and engaged in hot and often hasty words, a false step, the popping of a fire-cracker, an innocent gesture, might at once kindle a terrible flame." "Harrodsburg," *Louisville Courier-Journal*, January 8, 1874.

3. "Splendid passenger steamer" from "U.S. Mail Ohio Belle" advertisement, *New Orleans Daily Delta*, March 8, 1846. The advertisement added that the vessel had "unsurpassed accommodations."

1. A Splendid New Boat

1. "To the Public," *New Orleans Daily Crescent*, April 21, 1856; "River Intelligence," *Evansville Daily Journal*, March 14, 1856; "A Plucky Woman," *Rutland Weekly Herald*, January 30, 1873; Darrel E. Bigham, *Towns and Villages of the Lower Ohio* (Lexington: University Press of Kentucky, 1998): 75.

2. Sarah Chapin, "Edward Jarvis's Journal," *Filson Club History Quarterly* 70 (July 1996): 240; "The Very Latest News," *Nashville Union and American*, March 16, 1856; "Shocking Murder," *Evansville Daily Journal*, March 18, 1856; "Particulars of the Murder of Capt. Stevens," *Meigs County Telegraph*, March 25, 1856; "To the Public, *New Orleans Daily Crescent*, April 21, 1856; "A Plucky Woman," *Rutland Weekly Herald*, January 30, 1873.

3. Lewis Collins and Richard H. Collins, *History of Kentucky* (Salem, MA: Higginson Book, 1874), 1: 76; "The Very Latest News," *Nashville Union and American*, March 16, 1856; "Fatal Affray on a Boat—Clerk Shot," *Wheeling Daily Intelligencer*, March 17, 1856.

4. *Merchant Steam Vessels of the United States, 1807–1868* (Mystic, CT: Steamship Historical Society of America, 1953), 143; "Death of Capt. John Sebastian," *The Emporia News*, July 14, 1876.

5. James T. Lloyd, *Lloyd's Steamboat Directory and Disasters on the Western Waters* (Cincinnati: James T. Lloyd, 1856), 46; Robert Willis, "The Ohio River: A World-Class Inland Waterway," in Rita Kohn, ed. *Full Steam Ahead: Reflections on the Impact of the First Steamboat on the Ohio River, 1811–2011* (Indianapolis: Indiana Historical Society Press, 2011), 175; Adam I. Kane, *The Western River Steamboat* (College Station: Texas A&M University Press, 2004), 26, 30. For a history of Native American and early Anglo populations along the Ohio River, see Matthew Salafia, *Slavery's Borderland: Freedom and Bondage Along the Ohio River* (Philadelphia: University of Pennsylvania Press, 2013), 20–29.

6. Lloyd, *Lloyd's Steamboat Directory*, 49, 46; Kane, *Western River Steamboat*, 26; Chapin, *Edward Jarvis's Journal*, 245.

7. Zachary M. Bennett, "Improving Slavery's Border: Nature, Navigation, and Regionalism on the Ohio River," *The Register of the Kentucky Historical Society* 116 (Winter 2018): 15 (first quote), 1–2 (second quote); T. C. Purdy, "Report of Steam Navigation in the United States," *Report on the Agencies of Transportation in the United States* (Washington, DC: Government Printing Office, 1883), 12; David Herbert Donald, *Lincoln* (New York: Random House, 1995), 37–39; Carl Sandburg, *Abraham Lincoln: The Prairie Years and the War Years* (New York: Sterling Publishing 2007), 27; William O. Hubbard and Dennis Lee Taulbee, *Kentucky's Ohio River Boundary: From the Great Miami to the Wabash* (Frankfort, KY: Legislative Research Commission, 1972), 23; Kane, *Western River Steamboat*, 8–9; Lloyd, *Lloyd's Steamboat Directory*, 4; Chapin, "Edward Jarvis's Journal," 290. Michael Allen writes that "more than 200,000 men" worked on western flatboats during this period. Michael Allen, *Western Rivermen, 1763–1861: Ohio and Mississippi Boatmen and the Myth of the Alligator Horse* (Baton Rouge: Louisiana State University Press, 1990), 171.

8. Purdy, "Report of Steam Navigation," 12; Leland R. Johnson, "Harbinger of Revolution," in Kohn, *Full Steam Ahead*, 1, 14; Martha Kreipke, "The Falls of the Ohio and the Development of the Ohio River Trade, 1810–1860," *Filson Club History Quarterly* 54 (1980): 199; Kane, *Western River Steamboat*, 12; Lloyd, *Lloyd's Steamboat Directory*, 41. Historian Zach-

ary Bennett writes that "the introduction of the steamboat in 1811 . . . virtually collapsed the space between Louisville and New Orleans from four months to one week by 1828." Bennett, "Improving Slavery's Border," 5. Despite the advantages of steam travel, steamboats did not completely replace flatboats. Michael Allen writes that "flatboatmen flourished during most of the 1823–1861 period, controlling approximately 20 percent of the total inland river commerce." Lower costs and flatboats' ability to travel during the winter months contributed to their survival. Allen, *Western Rivermen*, 144.

9. Lloyd, *Lloyd's Steamboat Directory*, 42; Purdy, "Report of Steam Navigation," 12; Hubbard and Taulbee, *Kentucky's Ohio River Boundary*, 23.

10. Chapin, "Edward Jarvis's Journal," 234. George Rogers Taylor writes that from 1830 to 1860, "more than half of the Ohio and Mississippi steamboats were owned by from two to four men." George Rogers Taylor, *The Transportation Revolution, 1815–1860* (New York: M. E. Sharpe, 1951), 70.

11. Hubbard and Taulbee, *Kentucky's Ohio River Boundary*, 29, 30; Rick Bell, "The Era of Town Building Below the Falls," in Kohn, *Full Steam Ahead*, 63, 85; Willis, "The Ohio River, A World-Class Inland Waterway," in Kohn, *Full Steam Ahead*, 179; Kane, *Western River Steamboat*, 31; Kreipke, "Falls of the Ohio," 200; Bennett, "Improving Slavery's Border," 16; Taylor, *The Transportation Revolution*, 64. Bennett notes that commerce on the Ohio River was dependent on the weather. He writes, "The Ohio River was both the primary transportation corridor in the early American West and extremely unpredictable." Because inconsistent precipitation could keep the river shallow, Bennett adds, "The Ohio River was generally navigable by steamboats for only six months per year." Therefore, he notes, on the Ohio, "one of the nation's most important highways, nature still held sway." Bennett, "Improving Slavery's Border," 2–3.

12. Audubon quoted in Kohn, *Full Steam Ahead*, xii; Johnson, "Harbinger of Revolution," in Kohn, *Full Steam Ahead*, 1. For the Ohio River, migration, and the growth of the Trans-Appalachian west, see Christopher Phillips, *The Rivers Ran Backward: The Civil War and the Remaking of the American Middle Border* (Oxford: Oxford University Press, 2016), 22–25.

13. Kane, *Western River Steamboat*, 13, 18; Johnson, "Harbinger of Revolution," in Kohn, *Full Steam Ahead*, 1; Hubbard and Taulbee, *Kentucky's Ohio River Boundary*, 23; Kreipke, "Falls of the Ohio," 197. By the time of the Civil War, historian Larry J. Daniel writes, "Some 250 steamboats, one hundred freight barges, and two hundred coal barges plied the [Ohio] river daily, bringing vital commerce to Louisville and the 'Queen

City of the West,' Cincinnati, Ohio." Larry J. Daniel, *Days of Glory: The Army of the Cumberland, 1861–1865* (Baton Rouge: Louisiana State University Press, 2004), 4. For "urban growth" during the Steamboat Age, see also Allen, *Western Rivermen*, 141–143; and Kim M. Gruenwald, *River of Enterprise: The Commercial Origins of Regional Identity in the Ohio Valley, 1790–1850* (Bloomington: Indiana University Press, 2002), 82, 88, 116. For the importance of steamboats to the economies of Cincinnati and Louisville, see Gruenwald, *River of Enterprise*, 127–129, 116.

14. Kreipke, "The Falls of the Ohio," 197; Collins and Collins, *History of Kentucky*, 1: 36; population of Maysville from "Population of Maysville, KY," accessed via https://population.us/ky/maysville/ on 11 November 2018; Kane, *Western River Steamboat*, 13; "Steam is Crowding" from "American Steam Navigation," *Hunt's Merchant's Magazine* 4, (February 1841): 124; and quoted in Louis C. Hunter, *Steamboats on the Western Rivers: An Economic and Technological History* (New York: Dover Publications, 1977), 27.

15. Purdy, "Report of Steam Navigation," 13; Kreipke, "The Falls of the Ohio," 201, 215, 216; Kane, *Western River Steamboat*, 33; *Evansville Daily Journal*, January 20, 1857, 3; Hubbard and Taulbee, *Kentucky's Ohio River Boundary*, 23; Hunter, *Steamboats on the Western Rivers*, 321, 326.

16. Laura J. Davis, "Irregular Naval Warfare Along the Lower Mississippi," in Brian D. McKnight and Barton A. Myers, eds. *The Guerrilla Hunters: Irregular Conflicts During the Civil War* (Baton Rouge: Louisiana State University Press, 2017), 213; Hubbard and Taulbee, *Kentucky's Ohio River Boundary*, 24; Hunter, *Steamboats on the Western Rivers*, 287; Richard F. Selcer, *Civil War America, 1850 to 1875* (New York, Facts on File, 2006), 33; Mark Twain, *Life on the Mississippi* (New York: P. F. Collier and Son, 1874), 178. George Rogers Taylor notes that snags and underwater obstacles caused forty percent of steamboat losses from 1811–1851. He also writes that the average life of a steamboat was less than five years. Taylor, *The Transportation Revolution*, 65, 67.

17. Senator Snow quoted in "Terrible Disaster," *Chicago Tribune*, April 29, 1865. For the *Sultana* disaster, see Gene Eric Salecker, *Disaster on the Mississippi: The Sultana Explosion, April 27, 1865* (Annapolis, MD: Naval Institute Press, 1996); Alan Huffman, *Sultana: Surviving Civil War, Prison, and the Worst Maritime Disaster in American History* (New York: Harper Collins, 2009). For survivors' accounts, see Rev. Chester D. Berry, *Loss of the Sultana and Reminiscences of Survivors* (Lansing, MI: Darius D. Thorp, Printer: 1892).

18. Charles Dickens, *American Notes, Pictures from Italy, and a Child's*

History of England (London: Chapman and Hall, 1891), 125–126; Dickens also quoted in Kane, *Western River Steamboat*, xvii; E. W. Gould, *Fifty Years on the Mississippi, or, Gould's History of River Navigation* (St. Louis: Nixon-Jones Printing, 1889), 475–476; Lloyd, *Lloyd's Steamboat Directory*, 260–261.

19. Hunter, *Steamboats on the Western Rivers*, 101, 102; "that despicable stream" quoted in Mark Reinhardt, *Who Speaks for Margaret Garner? The True Story that Inspired Toni Morrison's Beloved* (Minneapolis: University of Minnesota Press, 2010), 174.

20. "Decapitated," *Sunbury American*, December 5, 1857.

21. "Shipping Intelligence," *The Baltimore Pilot*, April 22, 1840; Court of Claims Report, US House of Representatives, 35th Congress, 1st Session, Report C.C. No. 126, "James Thompson, Surviving Partner of C. M. Strader and Co.," *Report from the Court of Claims, Submitted to the House of Representatives During the First Session of the Thirty-Fifth Congress, 1857–58* (Washington, DC: James B. Steedman, 1858), 1: 113, 124, 138, 142, 143; *Commercial Advertiser and Journal*, November 12, 1839, 2; *Washington Madisonian*, July 1, 1841, 2; "Melancholy Accident," *New York Daily Tribune*, February 6, 1843.

22. *Whig Advocate*, May 16, 1840, 2. In July 1840, the *Ohio Belle* took another poll among passengers from seventeen states. The result was that 118 voters supported Harrison and twenty-five were for Van Buren. "Presidential Vote," *Yazoo Whig and Political Register*, July 10, 1840.

23. *Sentinel and Expositor for the Country*, May 10, 1842, 1.

24. "Steamer *Ohio Belle*," *New Orleans Times-Picayune*, February 2, 1840.

25. *Kimball and James' Business Directory for the Mississippi Valley: 1844* (Cincinnati: Kendall and Barnard, 1844): 55–56; *Haldeman's Picture of Louisville Directory and Business Advertiser for 1844–1845* (Louisville: Morning Courier Office, 1844), 159; D. Embree, *The Western Boatman, Devoted to Navigation, Containing a Steam Boat Directory and Registry of Pilots and Engineers* (Cincinnati: n.p., 1848), 199. Today's $642,000 figure calculated from https://westegg.com/inflation/, accessed online on March 24, 2018. George Rogers Taylor writes that the typical steamboat cost $20,000, while larger and more luxurious steamers cost from $40,000 to $60,000 or more. Taylor, *Transportation Revolution*, 69.

26. "For Nashville," *New Orleans Times-Picayune*, January 1, 1840; "For Nashville, Clarksville," *New Orleans Times-Picayune*, February 27, 1842; "Steamer Du Quesne," *New Orleans Times-Picayune*, May 29, 1842; "Petition of a Number of Captains of Steamboats and Others Interested

in the Navigation of the Western Rivers," *Public Documents Printed By Order of the Senate of the United States*, 28th Congress, 2nd Session (Washington, DC: Gales and Seaton, 1845), 2: 4; "And Yet Another," *New Orleans Times-Picayune*, November 6, 1841, 2; *New Orleans Times-Picayune*, January 19, 1842, 2; "River News," *Cincinnati Daily Press*, April 5, 1859; "Port of Louisville," *Louisville Morning Courier and American Democrat*, November 11, 1844; "Collision—Steamer Ohio Belle and Schooner Creole," *The Merchants' Magazine* 11 (November 1844): 459, 460; "Supreme Court of Louisiana, April Term, 1844," *The Western Law Journal*, 11: 517. It was reported that "the schooner struck the steamer head on, nearly at right angles, between the fore-hatchway and the boilers, and the starboard side; her bow was stove in, and she sunk very soon, while the steamer receiv'd no injury." "Collision," *Merchants' Magazine*, 459. McClain died in Cincinnati in 1867 of "softening of the brain," which would likely be dementia today. His obituary stated that "he also built and commanded the David White." From "Port Items," *Cincinnati Enquirer*, December 31, 1867.

27. Taylor theft noted in *Louisville Morning Courier*, February 17, 1845.

2. On the Other Side of the World

1. Tocqueville quoted in Walter Stahr, *Stanton: Lincoln's War Secretary* (New York: Simon and Schuster, 2017), 8. Tocqueville's journey also noted in Bennett, "Improving Slavery's Border," 3–4. Bennett writes that "the Ohio River was the largest contiguous slave boundary in the United States." Ibid., 2. See also Luke E. Harlow, *Religion, Race, and the Making of Confederate Kentucky, 1830–1880* (Cambridge: Cambridge University Press, 2014), 1–2. Matthew Salafia calls the Ohio River "an unstable divide between slavery and freedom throughout the antebellum period." Salafia, *Slavery's Borderland*, 1. Slave Henry Bibb called the Ohio River "an impassable gulf." Quoted in Ibid., 187.

2. 1860 Cincinnati population from "Table 9. Population of the 10 Largest Urban Places: 1860," accessed via https://www.census.gov/population/www/documentation/twps0027/tab09.txt on October 17, 2017; Phillips, *The Rivers Ran Backward*, 57; Kenneth H. Williams and James Russell Harris, eds. "Kentucky in 1860: A Statistical Overview," *The Register of the Kentucky Historical Society* 13 (Autumn 2005): 748. The stark difference in the Bluegrass region can be seen in Fayette County (Lexington), which had a population of 22,599 residents, 10,015 slaves, twelve hundred slave owners, and 96 free blacks. Bourbon County (Paris), also in central Kentucky, had 14,860 residents, 6,767 slaves, 858 slave

owners, and three hundred free blacks. Fayette County had 8.35 slaves per owner, whereas Bourbon County averaged 7.89. Williams and Harris, eds. "Kentucky in 1860," 748.

3. Phillips, *The Rivers Ran Backward*, 10; Salafia, *Slavery's Borderland*, 6. Support for slavery and black codes were certainly influenced by population statistics. Phillips writes, "In 1850 a full 41 percent of Indiana's entire population hailed from slave states (especially Kentucky and Tennessee), alongside about 30 percent of Illinois's population." Therefore, a solid percentage of the population came from states where slavery was legal. Ibid., 25. When Illinois became a state in 1818, one resident said that it was "as much a slave state as any south of the Ohio River." Quoted in Ibid., 32. Historian Luke Harlow also notes that "early American migrants into the Ohio Valley came from a variety of ideological persuasions, and they held conflicting views about the place slavery should occupy in the American nation. That conflict never waned: the region remained contested ground throughout the nineteenth century." Harlow, *Religion, Race, and the Making of Confederate Kentucky*, 1. For fugitive slaves and the Ohio River, see Salafia, *Slavery's Borderland*, 165–184.

4. "Salmon P. Chase and Negro Equality," *The Spirit of Democracy*, August 19, 1857, 2; Paul Finkleman, *Fugitive Slaves and American Courts: The Pamphlet Literature, Series 2, Volume 1* (Clark, NJ: The Lawbook Exchange, 2007), 236, 237; "The State v. Hoppess, in the Matter of Watson, Claimed as a Fugitive From Service," *Reports of Cases Argued and Determined in Ohio Courts of Record as Published in the Western Law Journal* (Norwalk, OH: Laning Printing, 1896), 2: 105, 106; Stephen Middleton, *The Black Laws: Race and the Legal Process in Early Ohio* (Athens: Ohio University Press, 2005), 185; "Samuel Watson," *Green Mountain Freeman*, February 28, 1845.

5. William Cooper, "James Gillespie Birney," in John E. Kleber, ed. *The Kentucky Encyclopedia* (Lexington: University Press of Kentucky, 1992), 82; Salafia, *Slavery's Borderland*, 199–201; Charles M. Spearman, "William Birney," in Patricia Faust, ed. *Historical Times Illustrated Encyclopedia of the Civil War* (New York: Harper Perennial, 1986), 61.

6. "Samuel Watson," *Green Mountain Freeman*, February 28, 1845; John E. Stanchak, "Salmon Portland Chase," in Faust, ed. *Historical Times Illustrated Encyclopedia*, 132; Middleton, *The Black Laws*, 185; Ezra J. Warner, *Generals in Blue: The Lives of the Union Commanders* (Baton Rouge: Louisiana State University, 1964), 304.

7. "Samuel Watson," *Green Mountain Freeman*, February 28, 1845; Middleton, *The Black Laws*, 185–86; "The State v. Hoppess," 2: 106; Fin-

kleman, *Fugitive Slaves*, 237, 238–239; Bennett, "Improving Slavery's Border," 14–15.

8. "Samuel Watson," *Green Mountain Freeman*, February 28, 1845, ("Have you done every thing" and "God Almighty bless you" also quoted); Middleton, *The Black Laws*, 186; Hunter, *Steamboats on the Western Rivers*, 239–240.

9. "The State v. Hoppess," 2: 279; Finkleman, *Fugitive Slaves*, 242; "Salmon P. Chase and Negro Equality," *The Spirit of Democracy*, August 19, 1857.

10. "Splendid passenger steamer" from "U.S. Mail Ohio Belle" advertisement, *New Orleans Daily Delta*, March 8, 1846.

11. "For New Orleans," *Louisville Morning Courier and American Democrat*, March 25, 1846; *Louisville Morning Courier*, December 15, 1846, 2; *Louisville Morning Courier*, December 19, 1846, 2; *Louisville Morning Courier*, February 8, 1847, 2; *Louisville Morning Courier*, November 8, 1847; "Army Intelligence," *New York Herald*, November 24, 1847; "Troops," *Washington Daily Union*, November 23, 1847; Executive Document No. 44, 13th Congress, 2nd Session, House of Representatives, Contracts Under Authority of the War Department, Letter from the Secretary of War (January 24, 1849), 36; "Arrival of Troops," *Washington Daily Union*, March 6, 1848; *Washington Weekly National Intelligencer*, March 4, 1848; *Louisville Morning Courier*, February 21, 1848, 2.

12. Advertisement, *New Orleans Daily Crescent*, March 25, 1848, 3.

13. S. W. Crittenden, *Book-Keeping By Single and Double Entry, Designed for Commercial Institutes, Private Students, and Practical Accountants* (Philadelphia: E. C. & J. Biddle, 1853), 34.

3. And the Mother Rejoiced

1. Arthur Wyllie, *The Confederate States Navy* (n.p., n.d., 2009), 171; Paul H. Silverstone, *Civil War Navies, 1855–1883* (New York: Routledge, 2006), 186, 195; Curtis A. Early and Gloria J. Early, *Ohio Confederate Connection* (NY: iUniverse, 2010), 195; *Official Records of the Union and Confederate Navies in the War of the Rebellion* (Washington, DC: Government Printing Office, 1908), ser. 1, vol. 22: 757 [hereinafter cited as *Naval OR*]; "At New Orleans," *Daily National Republican*, August 1, 1865; Lloyd, *Lloyd's Steamboat Directory*, 120; *Kimball and James' Business Directory for the Mississippi Valley: 1844* (Cincinnati: Kendall and Barnard, 1844), 49, 50; Hunter, *Steamboats on the Western Rivers*, 35; Erica Hannickel, *Empire of Vines: Wine Culture in America* (Philadelphia: University of Pennsylvania

Press, 2013), 97–98, 99 (Tocqueville quoted). Kim Gruenwald writes that the growth of Lexington, Kentucky—once known as "the Athens of the West"—was hindered because the city did not have a river. By 1830, Gruenwald explains, Cincinnati had bypassed Lexington "as the leader of cultural as well as economic development in the West." Gruenwald adds that "the transportation revolution [steamboats] elevated the role Louisville played in the region's economy, and Lexington found its prominent place gone." Gruenwald, *River of Enterprise*, 117, 144–145.

2. *Kimball and James' Business Directory*, 51, 55, 59, 62, 64, 67, 69, 71, 72, 73, 75, 76, 77, 78, 77, 78, 80, 93, 95, 96, 97, 98, 99, 107, 111, 114; Hannickel, *Empire of Vines*, 98; Hunter, *Steamboats on the Western Rivers*, 37; Lloyd, *Lloyd's Steamboat Directory*, 119.

3. Lloyd, *Lloyd's Steamboat Directory*, 119–120; Hunter, *Steamboat on the Western Rivers*, 106.

4. "Steamboat Departures," *New Orleans Daily Crescent*, January 29, 1856 (first quote); "River Intelligence," *New Orleans Daily Crescent*, December 20, 1859 (second quote); "Arrivals and Departures," *Evansville Daily Journal*, January 22, 1858; "Steamboat Departures," *New Orleans Daily Crescent*, January 29, 1856; "River News," *Evansville Daily Journal*, February 7, 1856; "River Intelligence," *Evansville Daily Journal*, December 7, 1855.

5. Benjamin F. Klein, ed. *The Ohio River Handbook and Picture Album* (Cincinnati: Young and Klein, 1969), 171; "Extract from Mr. Cist's book—'Cincinnati in 1841,'" *Cincinnati Enquirer*, April 17, 1841; "Local and River Brevities," *Evansville Daily Journal*, February 21, 1855; *Louisville Daily Courier*, March 2, 1855; *Louisville Daily Courier*, March 6, 1855; "Warming and Heating Stoves," *Baton Rouge Daily Comet*, January 3, 1856; "Local and River Brevities," *Evansville Daily Journal*, March 13, 1855; "Arrival of the Steam Fire-Engine," *New Orleans Daily Crescent*, July 14, 1855; "Mayoralty of New Orleans," *New Orleans Daily Crescent*, November 12, 1855; "River News," *Louisville Daily Courier*, July 6, 1855; "River Intelligence," *Evansville Daily Journal*, December 24, 1855.

6. George H. Devol, *Forty Years a Gambler on the Mississippi* (Bedford, MA: Applewood Books, reprint ed., 1887), 77.

7. Devol, *Forty Years a Gambler*, 77–78.

8. *Biographical and Historical Memoirs of Louisiana* (Chicago: Goodspeed Publishing, 1892), 2: 40; "To the Public," *New Orleans Daily Crescent*, April 21, 1856; "The Ohio Belle Tragedy," *Louisville Daily Courier*, April 11, 1856; "Steamboats," *Louisville Daily Courier*, March 10, 1855; "Steamboats," *Louisville Daily Courier*, January 16, 1855; 1860 US Federal Census,

Notes

Hamilton County, Ohio, Cincinnati, Ward 15 (accessed online via Ancestry.com on September 17, 2017); "Death of Capt. John Sebastian," *The Emporia News*, July 14, 1876; "Driftwood," *Louisville Courier-Journal*, July 14, 1876; 1850 US Federal Census, Campbell County, Kentucky, Newport City (accessed online via Ancestry.com on September 17, 2017). Genealogy from "John Sebastian, Early Colonial Settlers of Southern Maryland and Virginia's Northern Neck, www.colonial-settlers-md-va.us/getperson.php?personID=I040154&tree=tree1, accessed on December 7, 2017. Three brothers as steamboat pilots from "Registry of Pilots," *The Western Boatman* 1, January 1849.

9. Collins and Collins, *History of Kentucky*, 1: 76; "River Intelligence," *Evansville Daily Journal*, March 14, 1856.

10. "Steamboat Collision on the Ohio," *Richmond Daily Dispatch*, March 15, 1856; "Awful Steamboat Disaster," *Louisville Daily Courier*, March 10, 1856; "River Intelligence," *Evansville Daily Journal*, March 12, 1856.

11. Slaves crossing the icy Ohio River were also depicted in literature from the period. Historians Kim Gruenwald and Matthew Salafia note how Harriet Beecher Stowe used the frozen river in *Uncle Tom's Cabin* to allow the enslaved Eliza to escape across "the icy river to freedom." Gruenwald, *River of Enterprise*, xi; Salafia, *Slavery's Borderland*, 1. Although this was not referring to the "ice bridge" of 1856 (Stowe's book was first published in 1852), enslaved people crossing the frozen Ohio existed in both reality and the nation's popular imagination.

12. Owen Findsen, "Slaves' Case Ended in Tragedy," *Cincinnati Enquirer,* accessed online via enquirer.com/editions/2003/02/20/garner4.html on October 4, 2017; "Steamboat Collision on the Ohio," *Richmond Daily Dispatch*, March 15, 1856; "The Returned Slaves," *Anti-Slavery Bugle*, March 15, 1856; Francesca Gamber, "Margaret Garner," *Encyclopedia of African American History* (Santa Barbara: ABC-CLIO, 2010), 1: 422–424; Levi Coffin, *Reminiscences of Levi Coffin, The Reputed President of the Underground Railroad* (Cincinnati: Robert Clarke and Co., 1880), 560, 562–563 ("The babe she held" quote), 564 ("could see nothing" quote); "The Fugitives—The Requisition," *Western Reserve Chronicle*, March 19, 1856; Eric R. Jackson, "Margaret Garner," in Gerald L. Smith, Karen Cotton McDaniel, and John A. Hardin, eds. *The Kentucky African American Encyclopedia* (Lexington: University Press of Kentucky, 2015), 199; Salafia, *Slavery's Borderland*, 179–180. For information about Garner's owner, see Steven Weisenburger, *Modern Medea: A Family Story of Slavery and Child Murder from the Old South* (New York: Hill and Wang, 1998), 21–28.

Notes

13. Findsen, "Slaves' Case," *Cincinnati Enquirer;* "Steamboat Collision on the Ohio," *Richmond Daily Dispatch,* March 15, 1856; "Awful Steamboat Disaster," *Louisville Daily Courier,* March 10, 1856.

14. "Steamboat Collision on the Ohio," *Richmond Daily Dispatch,* March 15, 1856; "Awful Steamboat Disaster," *Louisville Daily Courier,* March 10, 1856.

15. "Steamboat Collision on the Ohio," *Richmond Daily Dispatch,* March 15, 1856; "Awful Steamboat Disaster," *Louisville Daily Courier,* March 10, 1856; Findsen, "Slaves' Case," *Cincinnati Enquirer.*

16. "Awful Steamboat Disaster," *Louisville Daily Courier,* March 10, 1856; Findsen, "Slaves' Case," *Cincinnati Enquirer.*

17. Findsen, "Slaves' Case," *Cincinnati Enquirer;* "Steamboat Collision on the Ohio," *Richmond Daily Dispatch,* March 15, 1856; "Awful Steamboat Disaster," *Louisville Daily Courier,* March 10, 1856; Gamber, *Margaret Garner,* 1: 424; Coffin, *Reminiscences of Levi Coffin,* 567; "The Returned Slaves," *Anti-Slavery Bugle,* March 15, 1856; "The Fugitives—The Requisition," *Western Reserve Chronicle,* March 19, 1856; "The Late Slave Case at Cincinnati," *Washington National Era,* March 20, 1856. Although some sources claimed that Garner was unshackled, it was also reported that she could not hold the baby because she was handcuffed. Therefore, Cilla's death could have been an accident, but it is more likely—considering her previous murder of her other daughter—that Garner let the baby drown. Reinhardt, *Who Speaks for Margaret Garner,* 136. It was also reported that Garner had struck the baby in the head with a shovel when authorities seized her in Cincinnati. "The Cincinnati Slaves—Another Thrilling Scene in the Tragedy," *The Liberator,* March 21, 1858.

18. "Steamboat Collision on the Ohio," *Richmond Daily Dispatch,* March 15, 1856; "Awful Steamboat Disaster," *Louisville Daily Courier,* March 10, 1856; Findsen, "Slaves' Case," *Cincinnati Enquirer;* "Steamboat Disaster—Loss of Life," *Washington National Era,* March 13, 1856; Reinhardt, *Who Speaks for Margaret Garner,* 135. The story of Marshal Butts's rescue from "The Cincinnati Slaves—Another Thrilling Scene in the Tragedy," *The Liberator,* March 21, 1858; "Butts and the Darkies," *Evansville Daily Journal,* March 13, 1856. Three months after the *Henry Lewis* sank, the "Submarine No. 7," a salvage vessel, pumped water out of the boat and raised it to the surface. The *Lewis* was then transported to Paducah, Kentucky, for repair. That October, the boat was "sold by a constable." "River Intelligence," *Evansville Daily Journal,* June 2, 1856; "Steamboat Sales," *Evansville Daily Journal,* September 27, 1856.

19. *Evansville Daily Journal,* March 10, 1856; Findsen, "Slaves' Case,"

Cincinnati Enquirer; Gamber, "Margaret Garner," 1: 424; Jackson, "Margaret Garner," 199.

20. Alberta Lewis Humble, "Matilda Agnes Heron," in Edward T. James, ed. *Notable American Women, 1607–1950: A Biographical Dictionary* (Cambridge, MA: The Belknap Press of Harvard University Press, 1971), 1: 187; Samuel French, trans. *Camille, or, The Fate of a Coquette* (New York: Samuel French, 1856), 2. French's translation was actually Matilda Heron's translation, which French published under his own name. Heron later forced him to publish a correction in later volumes.

21. Humble, "Matilda Agnes Heron," 1: 188; Thomas E. Garrett, *The Masque of the Muses* (St. Louis: St. Louis News, 1885), 39; James Fisher and Felicia Hardison Londre, "Emotional Actress," *The A to Z of American Theater* (Lanham, MD: Scarecrow Press, 2008), 154.

22. "Personal," *Washington Evening Star,* January 14, 1856; "St. Louis Theatre," *The Western Journal and Civilian,* February 1856; "The News," *Nashville Daily Patriot,* March 5, 1856; "Personal," *Washington Evening Star,* March 10, 1856; "Miss Matilda Heron," *Washington Sentinel,* March 20, 1856; "Editorial Melange," *Ballou's Pictorial Drawing Room Companion* 10, May 24, 1856; French, *Camille,* 2.

23. "Affray and Murder on a Steamboat," *New Orleans Daily Crescent,* March 21, 1856; "Murder and Probable Suicide on Board the Steamer Ohio Belle, *The Athens Post,* March 28, 1856; "Intelligent-Looking" from transcriptions of *Cairo Weekly Times,* "Murder on the Ohio Belle," https://pastisaforeignctountry.wordpress.com/2013/02/murder-aboard-the-ohio-belle/, accessed October 2, 2017; "The River Murder," *Louisville Weekly Courier,* April 12, 1856; "Shocking Murder," *Evansville Daily Journal,* March 18, 1856.

24. "Shocking Murder," *Evansville Daily Journal,* March 18, 1856; "To the Public," *New Orleans Daily Crescent,* April 21, 1856; "Affray and Murder on a Steamboat," *New Orleans Daily Crescent,* March 21, 1856; "A Plucky Woman," *Rutland Weekly Herald,* January 30, 1873; "Particulars of the Murder of Capt. Stevens," *Meigs County Telegraph,* March 25, 1856. Some newspaper reports incorrectly listed Stevens's name as "Ed. H. Stevens" or "Ed Stephens." In an article that Captain Sebastian later published, he named him as H. E. Stevens. "To the Public," *New Orleans Daily Crescent,* April 21, 1856. Stevens's internment record at Spring Grove Cemetery in Cincinnati lists him as Hiram E. Stevens. Internment Record for Hiram E. Stevens, Spring Grove Cemetery, accessed online at www.springgrove.org/stats/4913.tif.pdf.

25. "Affray and Murder on a Steamboat," *New Orleans Daily Cres-*

cent, March 21, 1856; "Steamboats," *Louisville Daily Courier,* July 15, 1854; "Steamboat Disaster," *Baton Rouge Gazette,* October 29, 1842; "Murdered for His Money," *Kansas City Journal,* September 26, 1897; "Steamboat Sunk," *Richmond Daily Dispatch,* April 21, 1854; *Louisville Daily Courier,* January 23, 1854; "Steamer Eliza Sunk," *Evansville Daily Journal,* February 1, 1855; "Steamboat Disaster—Great Loss of Life," *Richmond Daily Dispatch,* February 3, 1855; "Sinking of the Steamer Eliza," *Baton Rouge Weekly Comet,* February 4, 1855; "Unfounded Report," *Richmond Daily Dispatch,* February 10, 1855. For the murders perpetrated by the Kelleys, see D. L. Adair, *The Trial of Moses Kelley and Robert Kelley, Charged with the Murder of Alexander Gardner and Others* (Louisville: J. F. Brennan, 1853). When Stevens was captain of the *Eliza,* Stevens and the boat's owners sued two other steamers to reimburse them for costs incurred for towing them away from a burning steamboat. "Case No. 13,411, Stevens et al. v. The S. W. Downs & The Storm," *The Federal Cases Comprising Cases Argued and Determined in the Circuit and District Courts of the United States, Book 23* (St. Paul, MN: West Publishing, 1896): 34–35.

26. "To the Public," *New Orleans Daily Crescent,* April 21, 1856; "A Plucky Woman," *Rutland Weekly Herald,* January 30, 1873; "Shocking Murder," *Evansville Daily Journal,* March 18, 1856; "Particulars of the Murder of Capt. Stevens," *Meigs County Telegraph,* March 25, 1856; "The Very Latest News," *Nashville Union and American,* March 16, 1856; "Affray and Murder on a Steamboat," *New Orleans Daily Crescent,* March 21, 1856.

27. "To the Public," *New Orleans Daily Crescent,* April 21, 1856; "Particulars of the Murder of Capt. Stevens," *Meigs County Telegraph,* March 25, 1856 (Cincinnati paper quoted); "Murder and Probable Suicide on Board the Steamer Ohio Belle," *The Athens Post,* March 28, 1856; "The Very Latest News," *Nashville Union and American,* March 16, 1856; "Shocking Murder," *Evansville Daily Journal,* March 18, 1856; transcription of *Cairo Weekly Times.*

4. Boasting of the Bloody Deed

1. Historian Robert M. Ireland writes, "The habit of carrying deadly concealed weapons, combined with a hypersensitive notion of personal honor and a penchant for alcoholic beverages, formed a deadly social mix that resulted in many a fatal confrontation." Although Ireland's work focuses on Kentucky during this period, the same held true for violence on steamboats. Robert M. Ireland, "The Problem of Concealed Weapons in Nineteenth-Century Kentucky," *The Register of the Kentucky Historical*

Society 91 (Autumn 1993): 385. Violence also occurred on flatboats and keelboats. See Allen, *Western Rivermen*, 123–126.

2. H. Dwight Weaver, *Missouri Caves in History and Legend* (Columbia: University of Missouri Press, 2008), 47; Lowell H. Harrison and James C. Klotter, *A New History of Kentucky* (Lexington: University Press of Kentucky, 1997), 52; Helen Bartter Crocker, *The Green River of Kentucky* (Lexington: University Press of Kentucky, 2009), 6–7; James M. Prichard, "Blood Trail: Mass Murder on the Kentucky Frontier," *Kentucky Humanities* (April 2005): 3–8; Craig Thompson Friend, *Kentucke's Frontiers* (Bloomington: Indiana University Press, 2010), 211–212. For Cave-in-Rock and the Harpe brothers, also see Otto A. Rothert, *The Outlaws of Cave in Rock* (Carbondale, IL: Southern Illinois University Press, reprint ed., 1996).

3. Mary Wheeler, *Steamboatin' Days: Folk Songs of the River Packet Era* (Baton Rouge: Louisiana State University Press, 1944), 88, 104, 109.

4. Edward L. Ayers, *Vengeance and Justice: Crime and Punishment in the 19th Century American South* (New York: Oxford University Press, 1984), 14; "River and Steamboat Matters," *Memphis Daily Appeal*, March 27, 1861; "River Items," *Evansville Daily Journal*, March 27, 1861.

5. "For Cincinnati," *New Orleans Times Picayune*, January 3, 1864; "Port Items," *Cincinnati Enquirer*, April 3, 1869; "Port Items," *Cincinnati Enquirer*, May 7, 1869; "Cincinnati and the Red River Trade," *New Orleans Times Picayune*, February 14, 1871; "River Intelligence," *Cincinnati Enquirer*, November 28, 1872; "River News," *Pittsburgh Weekly Gazette*, March 1, 1873; "Correspondence," *Cincinnati Enquirer*, May 28, 1873; "Miscellaneous," *Memphis Public Ledger*, September 13, 1873; "River News," *St. Louis Dispatch*, May 15, 1874. "Charles Sebastian," Cave Hill Cemetery Burial Database, https://www.cavehillcemetery.com/search/, accessed December 7, 2017. In 1870 Charles Sebastian owned $4,000 in real estate in Louisville and lived with his family and several boarders, including steamboat pilot James A. Pell and a "Circus Actor," Charles Rivers. 1870 US Federal Census, Louisville, Jefferson County, Ward 4, accessed via Ancestry.com on December 7, 2017.

6. "Additional River Items," *Evansville Journal*, July 6, 1866.

7. "Eight Days Later from Rio Grande," *Louisville Morning Courier*, June 6, 1846; "Latest from the Rio Grande," *New York Daily Tribune*, June 8, 1846.

8. "Another Murder," *Louisville Morning Courier and American Democrat*, August 29, 1846; "A Murderer Recognized and Arrested," *New Orle-*

ans *Daily Crescent*, May 3, 1851; "Murder," *Southern Sentinel*, June 5, 1852; "Money Matters, &c.," *Richmond Daily Dispatch*, August 10, 1852; "Murderer Found," *Richmond Daily Dispatch*, August 11, 1852; "The Murder Case," *New Orleans Daily Crescent*, June 4, 1850.

9. "Murder Case," *Richmond Daily Dispatch*, March 28, 1853; "Murder on a Steamboat," *Gallipolis Journal*, September 29, 1853.

10. "The Detroit Murder," *Cleveland Morning Leader*, November 20, 1858.

11. "Arrest of the Supposed Murderers," *Wheeling Daily Intelligencer*, December 13, 1853; "The Murder on a Lake Erie Steamer," *New York Herald*, December 13, 1853; *Richmond Daily Dispatch*, December 23, 1853; "A Foul Murder," *The Weekly Comet*, September 30, 1855; "The Steamboat Murder," *New Orleans Daily Crescent*, January 18, 1856; *Pittsburgh Dispatch* from "News Items," *Nebraska Advertiser*, June 21, 1856.

12. *New York Daily Tribune*, February 14, 1856; "bowie knife and pistol gentry" from Little, *Ben Hardin*, 307. Regarding honor and reputation, Richard F. Hamm writes that "in antebellum southern society honor was a public commodity, conferred upon its recipient by the community and internalized by its holder." Richard F. Hamm, *Murder, Honor, and Law: 4 Virginia Homicides from Reconstruction to the Great Depression* (Charlottesville: University of Virginia Press, 2003), 21. Historian John Hope Franklin also recognizes that the South "institutionalized" violence "and bestowed upon it an aura of respectability" that was "sanctified by such time-honored institutions as the code duello, the militia muster, the military academy, the ring tournament, and the lynching party." John Hope Franklin, *The Militant South* (Chicago: The University of Illinois Press, 1956), ix.

13. Lorien Foote, *The Gentlemen and the Roughs: Violence, Honor, and Manhood in the Union Army* (New York: New York University Press, 2010), 83; Joanne B. Freeman, *Affairs of Honor: National Politics in the New Republic* (New Haven, CT: Yale University Press, 2001), 168; Hamm, *Murder, Honor, and Law*, 19. For the northern code of honor, see also Joanne B. Freeman, *The Field of Blood: Violence in Congress and the Road to Civil War* (New York: Farrar, Straus and Giroux, 2018), 71.

14. Russell quoted in Franklin, *The Militant South*, 39; Alabama editor quoted in Ibid., 60; Little, *Ben Hardin*, 290; "A Very Famous Trial," *Weekly Clarion-Ledger*, January 29, 1903; "A Wedding Tragedy," *Louisville Courier-Journal*, November 16, 1884. In his assessment of southern violence, historian John Hope Franklin writes that "no Southern state was more

subservient to the 'Bloody Code' than Mississippi." Moreover, Franklin notes planters' sons in the "Memphis region," including Jones's native Holly Springs, Mississippi, who wore "their honor 'on their sleeves.'" Franklin, *The Militant South*, 38, 43.

15. Freeman, *Field of Blood*, 218–225; William W. Freehling, *The Road to Disunion: Secessionists Triumphant, 1854–1861* (New York: Oxford University Press, 2007), 79–84; Franklin, *The Militant South*, 55.

16. James C. Klotter, *Kentucky Justice, Southern Honor, and American Manhood: Understanding the Life and Death of Richard Reid* (Baton Rouge: Louisiana State University Press, 2003), 48; Bertram Wyatt-Brown, *Southern Honor: Ethics and Behavior in the Old South* (New York: Oxford University Press, 2007), 360, 350, 400; John Mayfield, "The Marketplace of Values: Honor and Enterprise in the Old South," in John Mayfield and Todd Hagstette, eds. *The Field of Honor: Essays on Southern Character and American Identity* (Columbia: University of South Carolina Press, 2017), 5. Historian Dick Steward writes, "Southern individualism, nurtured by isolationism, provincialism, and suspicion of government and law, promoted a call to arms in defense of honor." He adds that duels and honor culture "romanticized the martial spirit and indoctrinated the populace into believing that violence was an acceptable means of problem solving." Dick Steward, *Duels and the Roots of Violence in Missouri* (Columbia: University of Missouri Press, 2000), 8, 208.

17. Klotter, *Kentucky Justice*, 49; Franklin, *The Militant South*, 34; Ayers, *Vengeance and Justice*, 19, 13; Hamm, *Murder, Honor, and Law*, 22; Dickson D. Bruce, *Violence and Culture in the Antebellum South* (Austin: University of Texas Press, 1979), 79. Historian Lorien Foote writes that southern men of all classes adhered to the code of honor, but "men from different social classes in the south manifested honor through different rituals." Foote writes that "the duel was reserved for gentlemen and rising young professionals." Only gentlemen dueled "because supposedly only men of high social status had carefully cultivated the ability to channel and control passion." Foote adds that "southern men from the lowest socioeconomic classes also had honor, but they satisfied their peers' demands through brutally violent rituals such as rough and tumble fighting," which had no rules. Therefore, had Jones been insulted by a member of the planter elite, instead of by a lower-class clerk, Jones possibly would have issued a challenge to duel, as opposed to immediately killing Stevens. His drunkenness, and the fact he was on the run from the law also influenced his decision to respond with violence rapidly. Foote, *The Gentlemen and the Roughs*, 96, 78.

5. Not the First Man I've Killed

1. "Particulars of the Murder of Capt. Stevens," *Meigs County Telegraph*, March 25, 1856; "To the Public," *New Orleans Daily Crescent*, April 21, 1856; transcriptions of the *Cairo Weekly Times*.

2. "Particulars of the Murder of Capt. Stevens," *Meigs County Telegraph*, March 25, 1856; "Shocking Murder," *Evansville Daily Journal*, March 18, 1856; transcriptions of the *Cairo Weekly Times*; "Southern Crimes and Horrors," *The Liberator*, May 2, 1856.

3. "The Ohio Belle Tragedy," *The Winchester Appeal*, April 5, 1856; "To the Public," *New Orleans Daily Crescent*, April 21, 1856; "The Ohio Belle Tragedy," *The Winchester Appeal*, April 5, 1856.

4. "A Shocking Scene in the West," *Wheeling Daily Intelligencer*, April 3, 1856; "The Ohio Belle Tragedy," *The Winchester Appeal*, April 5, 1856. Sebastian wrote that Jones was tied "to a stancheon [*sic*] in the engine room aft the boilers." "To the Public," *New Orleans Daily Crescent*, April 21, 1856.

5. "He's not the first man I've killed" and "one of the many desperadoes" from "Particulars of the Murder of Capt. Stevens," *Meigs County Telegraph*, March 25, 1856; Ayers, *Vengeance and Justice*, 14.

6. "A Shocking Scene in the West," *Wheeling Daily Intelligencer*, April 3, 1856; "The Ohio Belle Affair," *Louisville Daily Courier*, April 7, 1856; Dickson D. Bruce Jr., *The Kentucky Tragedy: A Story of Conflict and Change in Antebellum America* (Baton Rouge: Louisiana State University Press, 2006), 101, 102. For the Beauchamp-Sharp killing, see also Matthew G. Schoenbachler, *Murder and Madness: The Myth of the Kentucky Tragedy* (Lexington: University Press of Kentucky, 2009).

7. Hunter, *Steamboats on the Western Rivers*, 410–412. Various crimes also occurred on keelboats and flatboats. See Allen, *Western Rivermen*, 131–133.

8. Chapin, "Edward Jarvis's Journal," 291; "Three Thieves Lynched," *Louisville Daily Courier*, April 20, 1857; "Lynch Law," *Washington Daily Republic*, July 27, 1853; "Railroad Accident—Negro Lynched," *Memphis Daily Appeal*, April 15, 1857; "By Telegraph," *The Ottawa Free Trader*, September 28, 1849; "Steamboat Accidents," *Washington Daily Union*, September 29, 1849. Examples of "lynched" not meaning a hanging include the headlines "Three Thieves Lynched," *Louisville Daily Courier*, April 20, 1857 and "Lynch Law," *Washington Daily Republic*, July 27, 1853.

9. "Lynch Law—Probable Murder," *Anti-Slavery Bugle*, August 4, 1855.

Notes

10. Bennett, "Improving Slavery's Border," 10–11. Flatboatmen also engaged in mob violence. Michael Allen writes that this included "protests, sometimes violent, over the passage of wharf regulations and taxes in the hitherto unregulated river towns of the lower Mississippi." In his study of western rivermen, Allen notes riots at Natchez-Under-the-Hill in 1837 and a riot over "a heavy wharf tax" at St. Francisville, Louisiana, and Memphis in the 1840s. But, Allen notes, these included "not much action." Allen, *Western Rivermen*, 197, 199, 200–202.

11. Ann Hassenpflug, "Murder in the Classroom: Privilege, Honor, and Cultural Violence in Antebellum Louisville," *Ohio Valley History* 4 (Summer 2004): 5, 8, 10, 11–13, 16; "Mob in Louisville," *The Indiana Herald*, May 10, 1854; Robert M. Ireland, "Matthew Ward Trial," *Kentucky Encyclopedia*, 928. For a full accounting of the trial, see George Cole, *Trial of Matt. F. Ward for the Murder of Prof. W. H. G. Butler, Before the Hardin Criminal Court, April Term 1854* (Louisville: Morton and Griswold, 1854).

12. George H. Yater, "Bloody Monday," *The Kentucky Encyclopedia*, 88–89; Leslie Ann Harper, "Lethal Language: The Rhetoric of George Prentice and Louisville's Bloody Monday," *Ohio Valley History* (Fall 2011): 24; David L. Baker, "The Joyce Family Murders: Justice and Politics in Know-Nothing Louisville," *The Register of the Kentucky Historical Society* 102 (Summer 2004): 360–361.

13. "The Late Murder and Arson in the County," *Louisville Daily Courier*, December 24, 1856; "Shocking Affair," *Louisville Daily Courier*, December 22, 1856; "A Family Murdered in Kentucky," *New Orleans Times-Picayune*, December 23, 1856; "News Summary," *Brooklyn Evening Star*, December 23, 1856; "Sequel to the Late Tragedy," *Louisville Daily Courier*, May 16, 1857; "A Mysterious and Tragic Affair—Suspected Murder, Arson, and Robbery," *Kentucky Tribune*, December 26, 1856. For an overview of the incident, see Baker, "The Joyce Family Murders," 357–382.

14. "Examination of the Four Slaves for Murder and Arson—their Committal," *Louisville Daily Courier*, December 29, 1856; "Jefferson Circuit Court," *Louisville Daily Courier*, January 16, 1857; "Murder of the Joyce Family," *The Liberator*, April 3, 1857; "The Late Murder and Arson in the County," *Louisville Daily Courier*, December 24, 1856; Baker, "The Joyce Family Murders," 365; "a hand axe" from "The Late Murder and Arson in the County," *Louisville Daily Courier*, December 24, 1856.

15. "Terrible Tragedy!!!" *Louisville Daily Courier*, May 15, 1857; "The Mob of Last Evening," *Louisville Daily Courier*, May 15, 1857; Baker, "The Joyce Family Murders," 366, 369.

Notes

16. "Terrible Tragedy!!!" *Louisville Daily Courier*, May 15, 1857; Baker, "The Joyce Family Murders," 371.

17. "The Mob of Last Evening," *Louisville Daily Courier*, May 15, 1857; Louisville resident from "The Courier and the Late Mob," *Louisville Daily Courier*, May 23, 1857; "The Late Mob," *Louisville Daily Courier*, June 1, 1857; Baker, "The Joyce Family Murders," 378, 381; "Our Outside Pages," *Louisville Daily Courier*, October 3, 1857.

18. Harper, "Lethal Language," 26; Bruce, *Violence and Culture in the Antebellum South*, 82–83. Bruce adds that most vigilantes were "plainfolk." Ibid., 110–111.

19. "Shocking Murder," *Evansville Daily Journal*, March 18, 1856.

20. Willis, "The Ohio River," *Full Steam Ahead*, 175; Chapin, "Edward Jarvis's Journal," 296–297.

21. "To the Public," *New Orleans Daily Crescent*, April 21, 1856; Bruce, *Violence and Culture in the Antebellum South*, 85–86; Jackson's mother quoted in Ayers, *Vengeance and Justice*, 18.

22. "To the Public," *New Orleans Daily Crescent*, April 21, 1856; "A Shocking Scene in the West," *Wheeling Daily Intelligencer*, April 3, 1856; "The Ohio Belle Tragedy," *The Winchester Appeal*, April 5, 1856; "Affray and Murder on a Steamboat," *New Orleans Daily Crescent*, March 21, 1856; "The Ohio Belle Tragedy," *Louisville Daily Courier*, April 11, 1856.

23. Surprisingly, Stevens's internment record at Spring Grove Cemetery in Cincinnati notes that he was buried there on April 16, nearly a month after he was killed. On that date, he was buried in section 45, lot 7, which was owned by Henry A. Jones, who had hosted Stevens's funeral. It is possible that Stevens was initially buried in northern Kentucky (the *Evansville Daily Journal* contended that his funeral was held in Newport) or placed in a vault in Cincinnati before being interred in Jones's lot. Regardless, nearly ten years later, on November 11, 1867, Stevens's remains were again reinterred at Spring Grove in section 27, lot 21, space 3. It is unknown why his body was moved. Stevens internment record, Spring Grove Cemetery. Jones was a steamboat captain who purchased the *Jesse K. Bell* in 1859. "River Intelligence," *Cincinnati Daily Press*, February 23, 1859. By 1870, Jones was president of the Memphis and Cincinnati Packet Company. *Williams Cincinnati Directory* (Cincinnati: Cincinnati Directory Office, 1870), 424. For a biographical note on Jones, see Richard F. Miller, ed. *States At War, Volume 5, A Reference Guide for Ohio in the Civil War* (Lebanon, NH: University Press of New England, 2015), 382 n32.

24. "Particulars of the Murder of Capt. Stevens," *Meigs County Telegraph*, March 25, 1856; *Louisville Daily Courier*, March 17, 1856; "Foul

Murder," *Louisville Daily Courier*, March 17, 1856; "River Intelligence," *Evansville Daily Journal*, March 20, 1856; "Shocking Murder," *Evansville Daily Journal*, March 18, 1856; *Cincinnati Commercial* quoted in *New Orleans Times-Picayune*, March 26, 1856. The *Chicago Tribune* reported that Stevens's funeral "takes place at 2 o'clock from the residence of Capt. H. A. Jones, 82 Pike street. The Odd Fellows of which he was a member, will attend." "Shocking Murder," *Chicago Tribune*, March 20, 1856. On July 1, 1844, Stevens married Wealthy Ann White in Cincinnati. "Ohio, County Marriages, 1774–1993," accessed via Ancestry.com on November 7, 2017.

25. "Shocking Murder," *Evansville Daily Journal*, March 18, 1856; "The Ohio Belle Affair," *Evansville Daily Journal*, April 8, 1856.

26. "The Ohio Belle Tragedy," *Louisville Daily Courier*, April 7, 1856; "To the Public," *New Orleans Daily Crescent*, April 21, 1856.

27. "To the Public," *New Orleans Daily Crescent*, April 21, 1856; "The Ohio Belle Tragedy," *Louisville Daily Courier*, April 7, 1856; "The Ohio Belle Tragedy," *Louisville Daily Courier*, January 13, 1858.

28. "To the Public," *New Orleans Daily Crescent*, April 21, 1856; "The Ohio Belle Tragedy," *Louisville Daily Courier*, April 11, 1856; "The Ohio Belle Tragedy," *Louisville Daily Courier*, January 16, 1858; "Murder and Probable Suicide on Board the Steamer Ohio Belle," *The Athens Post*, March 28, 1856; "Reported Drowned," *Louisville Daily Courier*, March 18, 1856; "Affray and Murder on a Steamboat," *New Orleans Daily Crescent*, March 21, 1856.

29. Transcriptions of *Cairo Weekly Times*; "The Ohio Belle Affair," *Evansville Daily Journal*, April 8, 1856.

30. "The Ohio Belle Affair," *Louisville Weekly Courier*, April 12, 1856; transcripts of the *Cairo Weekly Times*; "The Ohio Belle Affair," *Evansville Daily Journal*, April 8, 1856.

6. A Man of Property

1. "The Ohio Belle Tragedy," *Louisville Daily Courier*, January 13, 1858; "Southern Crimes and Horrors," *The Liberator*, May 2, 1856; "The Ohio Belle Affair," *Louisville Daily Courier*, April 7, 1856.

2. "Affray on Steamer Ohio Belle," *Daily Louisville Democrat*, March 17, 1856; *Louisville Daily Courier*, March 17, 1856; "The Ohio Belle Affair," *Louisville Daily Courier*, April 7, 1856; "Close of a Tragedy," *Richmond Daily Dispatch*, April 11, 1856; St. Louis paper quoted in "A Horrible Tragedy," *Thibodaux Minerva*, April 12, 1856; *Memphis Eagle* quoted in "The Ohio Belle Affair," *Evansville Daily Journal*, April 18, 1856.

Notes

3. "The Ohio Belle Affair," *Evansville Daily Journal*, April 8, 1856.

4. *Columbus* (KY) *Citizen* quoted in "The Ohio Belle Affair," *Evansville Daily Journal*, April 8, 1856; "The Ohio Belle Affair," *Louisville Weekly Courier*, April 12, 1856.

5. "To the Public," *New Orleans Daily Crescent*, April 21, 1856; "The Ohio Belle Tragedy," *Louisville Daily Courier*, April 11, 1856. In addition to sometimes being attacked by insulted readers, editors also participated in formal duels. See Jack K. Williams, *Dueling in the Old South: Vignettes of Social History* (College Station: Texas A&M University Press, 1980), 29–33. Historian John Hope Franklin examines a number of editors who dueled or engaged in street fights, writing that "no class of Southerner, perhaps, went to the field of honor more frequently than newspaper editors." John Hope Franklin, *The Militant South: 1800–1861* (Chicago: University of Illinois Press, 2002), 55–58.

6. *Memphis Eagle* quoted in "The Ohio Belle Affair," *Evansville Daily Journal*, April 8, 1856; "Singular Development," *The Panola Star*, April 12, 1856.

7. *Memphis Eagle* quoted in "The Ohio Belle Affair," *Evansville Daily Journal*, April 8, 1856. Multiple newspapers reported that Cocke's father went through Memphis to retrieve his son's remains. *New Orleans Daily Crescent*, April 10, 1856; "Singular Development," *The Panola Star*, April 12, 1856.

8. Bruce, *Violence and Culture in the Antebellum South*, 76.

9. 1850 US Federal Census—Slave Schedule—Marshall County, Mississippi, Northern District, accessed via Ancestry.com on September 13, 2017; "Joseph Cock," Find-A-Grave Memorial #11545074, accessed via FindAGrave.com on September 13, 2017; 1850 US Federal Census, Marshall County, Mississippi, Northern Division, accessed via Ancestry.com on September 13, 2017; 1860 US Federal Census—Slave Schedule—Marshall County, Mississippi, Township 3, Range 1 & 2 West, accessed via Ancestry.com on September 13, 2017; "George Washington Cock," Find-A-Grave Memorial #36422336, accessed via FindAGrave.com on September 13, 2017.

10. "Public Barbeque at Holly Springs," *Mississippi Palladium*, August 14, 1851; "Democratic Meeting," *The Guard*, May 29, 1845.

11. "Arrest of a Murderer," *Richmond Daily Dispatch*, January 23, 1854; "Another," *New Orleans Daily Crescent*, December 11, 1851; "Awful Tragedy," *The Primitive Republican*, December 11, 1851; 1850 US Federal Census, Marshall County, Mississippi, Northern Division, accessed via Ancestry.com on September 13, 2017.

Notes

12. *Holly Springs Jeffersonian* quoted in "Awful Tragedy," *The Primitive Republican*, December 11, 1851.

13. "Awful Tragedy," *The Primitive Republican*, December 11, 1851; 1850 US Federal Census, Marshall County, Mississippi, Northern Division, accessed online via Ancestry.com on September 13, 2017; 1860 US Federal Census—Slave Schedule—Marshall County, Mississippi, accessed via Ancestry.com on September 13, 2017; 1860 US Federal Census, Marshall County, Mississippi, accessed via Ancestry.com on September 13, 2017; "Arrest of a Murderer," *Richmond Daily Dispatch*, January 23, 1854; *Washington Daily Union*, March 30, 1854: 3; "Arrest of a Murderer," *New York Herald*, April 9, 1854.

14. Todd Hagstette, "Writing the Duel: Rhetorical Negotiation and the Language of Honor in the Nineteenth-Century South," in Mayfield and Hagstette, ed. *The Field of Honor,* 80; Bruce, *Violence and Culture in the Antebellum South,* 41. Richard F. Hamm writes that "wealth, individual and family, was important in establishing a man's status as a gentlemen [*sic*] (and all gentlemen were presumed to be honorable)." Hamm, *Murder, Honor, and Law,* 20.

15. "In well-bred Society," quoted in Freeman, *Affairs of Honor,* 170–171; Bruce, *Violence and Culture in the Antebellum South,* 53; Wyatt-Brown, *Southern Honor,* 351–352; "almost any man of spirit," from *Columbus* (KY) *Citizen* quoted in "The Ohio Belle Affair," *Evansville Daily Journal,* April 8, 1856, and quoted in "The Ohio Belle Affair," *Louisville Weekly Courier,* April 12, 1856. On alcohol leading to "passions . . . out of control" and violence, see Bruce, *Violence and Culture in the Antebellum South,* 74–75.

16. Randolph quoted in Bruce, *Violence and Culture in the Antebellum South,* 56. Historian John Hope Franklin also assesses this facet of southerners' character. Franklin notes that "the feeling of personal responsibility in defending himself, together with the deep appreciation for the idea of honor, created in each Southerner a sense of 'personal sovereignty.' Ruler of his own destiny, defender of his own person and honor, he approached a personal imperiousness that few modern men have achieved." Franklin, *The Militant South,* 36.

17. Hamm, *Murder, Honor, and Law,* 19; Bruce, *Violence and Culture in the Antebellum South,* 66, 65, 67; "the foundation" quoted in Franklin, *The Militant South,* 67–68. Bruce also notes A. B. Longstreet, who wrote that southerners were "quick of temper, sensitive to insult, and too quick to revenge it." Quoted in Bruce, *Violence and Culture in the Antebellum South,* 70. For more on slavery influencing southern violence, see Ayers, *Vengeance and Justice,* 10–11, 25–27.

Notes

18. Franklin, *The Militant South*, 69.

19. Bruce, *Violence and Culture in the Antebellum South*, 65, 71; Bruce, *The Kentucky Tragedy*, 100.

20. "The Ohio Belle Affair," *Evansville Daily Journal*, April 8, 1856; "The Ohio Belle Affair," *Louisville Daily Courier*, April 7, 1856; "Capt. Sebastian Indicted," *Louisville Daily Courier*, April 30, 1856; "The River Murder," *Louisville Weekly Courier*, April 12, 1856; "River Intelligence," *Evansville Daily Journal*, May 3, 1856; transcriptions of the *Cairo Weekly Times*.

21. "Marble Receipts," *Evansville Daily Journal*, May 9, 1856; "River Intelligence," *Evansville Daily Journal*, May 8, 1856; "River Intelligence," *Evansville Daily Journal*, May 12, 1856; "Canal at the Falls—Meeting of Steamboatmen," *Louisville Daily Courier*, July 2, 1856; "The Canal," *Louisville Daily Courier*, October 29, 1856; "River, &c.," *Daily Louisville Times*, December 12, 1856; "Steamboat Departures this Day," *New Orleans Daily Crescent*, June 29, 1857.

22. *Louisville Daily Courier*, March 17, 1857: 1; *Louisville Daily Courier*, March 16, 1857: 1; *Louisville Daily Courier*, March 19, 1857: 1; "River News," *Wheeling Daily Intelligencer*, April 22, 1857.

23. *Evansville Daily Journal*, February 8, 1858; "The Ohio Belle Tragedy," *Louisville Daily Courier*, January 13, 1858; "The Ohio Belle Tragedy," *Louisville Daily Courier*, January 16, 1858.

24. *Louisville Daily Courier*, November 6, 1858: 4; E. W. Gould, *Fifty Years on the Mississippi* (St. Louis, Nixon-Jones Printing, 1889), 369.

25. "River Intelligence," *Cincinnati Daily Press*, March 1, 1859; "River Intelligence," *Cincinnati Daily Press*, March 18, 1859. Michael Allen writes that "by 1853, Cincinnati boasted direct rail connections with the East, and its river trade suffered acutely." Allen, *Western Rivermen*, 168. Despite this, business on the *Belle* continued to be good. In April 1859, the steamboat reached Cincinnati "with a full load." "Arrivals and Departures," *Cincinnati Daily Press*, April 20, 1859.

26. "Receipts of Produce," *New Orleans Daily Crescent*, March 19, 1860; "Receipts of Produce," *New Orleans Daily Crescent*, December 10, 1860. For Cincinnati commerce at the beginning of the Civil War, see William Smith, *Annual Statement of the Commerce of Cincinnati, for the Commercial Year, Ending Aug. 31, 1861, Reported to the Chamber of Commerce* (Cincinnati: Gazette Company Steam Printing, 1861). The *Arabia*, a steamboat that sank on the Missouri River in 1856, a few months after Jones killed Stevens on the *Ohio Belle*, was rediscovered in 1987. The contents of the *Arabia* are now preserved at the Arabia Steamboat Museum in Kansas City, providing a lens into the variety and quality of goods carried aboard

steamboats during that period. See "Arabia's Story," accessed from http://1856.com/arabias-story/ on November 4, 2018.

27. "Workhoused," *New Orleans Daily Crescent*, December 20, 1859.

7. Oh! The Horrors of War

1. "US Senate Report to Accompany Bill 5855, US Congress, 49th Session, Report No. 1329," *Reports of Committees of the Senate of the United States for the First Session of the Forty-Ninth Congress, 1885–1886* (Washington, DC: Government Printing Office, 1886), 10: 2; "River Intelligence," *New Orleans Daily Crescent*, February 5, 1861; "Receipts of Produce," *New Orleans Daily Crescent*, February 5, 1861; "Fires," *Cincinnati Daily Press*, March 25, 1861. Benjamin F. Cooling writes that "traffic on the Ohio River, depressed during the secession year, revived following the winter and spring victories of the Federals in 1862." He adds that river traffic dropped again in the autumn of 1862, as Confederate armies advanced into Kentucky. However, by "1863 onward, war business boomed." Benjamin Franklin Cooling, *To the Battles of Franklin and Nashville and Beyond: Stabilization and Reconstruction in Tennessee and Kentucky, 1864–1866* (Knoxville: University of Tennessee Press, 2011), 26.

2. "River Items," *Evansville Daily Journal*, April 16, 1861; "River Intelligence," *New Orleans Daily Crescent*, April 22, 1861. For Lincoln's call for seventy-five thousand troops, see William C. Harris, *Lincoln and the Border States: Preserving the Union* (Lawrence: University Press of Kansas, 2011), 39; Williamson Murray and Wayne Wei-Siang Hsieh, *A Savage War: A Military History of the Civil War* (Princeton, NJ: Princeton University Press, 2016), 73–74; James M. McPherson, *Battle Cry of Freedom: The Civil War Era* (New York: Ballantine Books, 1988), 274.

3. "News from the South," *Washington Evening Star*, April 27, 1861; "Seizure of the Westmoreland," *Shreveport Daily News*, May 3, 1861.

4. "The War Excitement at Cairo," *Shreveport Southwestern*, May 8, 1861.

5. "Affairs on the Mississippi River," *Richmond Daily Dispatch*, May 3, 1861; Chapin, "Edward Jarvis's Journal," 292.

6. *Journal of Both Sessions of the Convention of the State of Arkansas* (Little Rock, AR: Johnson and Yerkes, 1861), 151–152, 267–268; A. C. Denson, *Westmoreland; or, Secession Ferocity at the Breaking Out of the Rebellion* (St. Louis: P. M. Pinckard, 1865), 8, 9; "Affairs on the Mississippi River," *Richmond Daily Dispatch*, May 3, 1861; "Local Matters," *Memphis Daily Appeal*, April 30, 1861; *Daily Nashville Patriot*, May 1, 1861, 3.

7. "US Senate Report to Accompany Bill S855," *Reports of Committees of the Senate*, 2; "From the Mississippi Flotilla," *New York Daily Tribune*, July 11, 1862.

8. "Seizure of the Westmoreland," *Shreveport Daily News*, May 3, 1861; "Affairs on the Mississippi River," *Richmond Daily Dispatch*, May 3, 1861; Denson, *Westmoreland*, 10; "$175,000 Worth of Tennessee Arms and Ammunition Stolen!" *Richmond Enquirer*, May 3, 1861.

9. "Seizure of the Westmoreland," *Shreveport Daily News*, May 3, 1861; "Affairs on the Mississippi River," *Richmond Daily Dispatch*, May 3, 1861; "Another Steamboat Seized," *Yorkville Enquirer*, May 14, 1861.

10. "From the Mississippi Flotilla," *New York Daily Tribune*, July 11, 1862.

11. *Louisville Daily Courier*, April 30, 1861.

12. *Daily Nashville Patriot*, May 1, 1861, 3; "Affairs on the Mississippi River," *Richmond Daily Dispatch*, May 3, 1861; "Letter from Cairo," *Chicago Daily Tribune*, May 7, 1861; "Local Brevities," *Cincinnati Daily Star*, July 12, 1876.

13. "River Intelligence," *New Orleans Daily Crescent*, July 2, 1861; "US Senate Report to Accompany Bill S855," *Reports of Committees of the Senate*, 2; "From Cairo," *Louisville Daily Courier*, May 11, 1861; "Reign of Terror in Memphis," *Chicago Daily Tribune*, May 15, 1861; US War Department, *The War of the Rebellion: A Compilation of the Official Records of the Union and Confederate Armies* (US Government Printing Office, 1880–1901), vol. 8: 800 [hereinafter cited as *OR*. Unless noted, all references refer to Series I]; *Naval OR*, ser. 1, vol. 22: 742; Early and Early, *Ohio Confederate Connection*, 195; "For the Seat of War," *Memphis Daily Appeal*, July 17, 1861; Duane Huddleston, Sammie Cantrell Rose, and Pat Taylor Wood, *Steamboats and Ferries on the White River: A Heritage Revisited* (Fayetteville: University of Arkansas Press, 1998), 50; Loreta Janeta Velazquez, *The Woman in Battle: A Narrative of the Exploits, Adventures, and Travels of Madame Loreta Janeta Velazquez, Otherwise Known As Lieutenant Harry T. Buford, Confederate States Army* (Richmond, Dustin, Gilman 1876), 85; "River and Steamboat Matters," *Memphis Daily Appeal*, September 7, 1861. William C. Davis, "Confederate Con Artist," *Civil War Times*, June 2017, accessed online via http://www.historynet.com/confederate-con-artist.htm on March 24, 2018; see also William C. Davis, *Inventing Loreta Velasquez: Confederate Soldier Impersonator, Media Celebrity, and Con Artist* (Bloomington, Southern Illinois Press, 2016).

14. "A Card," *Memphis Daily Appeal*, August 15, 1861; *OR*, vol. 8: 693; "For Little Rock," *Memphis Public Ledger*, May 7, 1870. The forty-nine-

year-old John J. Edson died in Memphis of pneumonia or consumption in January 1879. "Local Paragraphs," *Memphis Daily Appeal*, January 26, 1879. Born in Kentucky, Edson was buried in Elmwood Cemetery in Memphis. "Capt. John J. Edson," Find-A-Grave memorial no. 116032726, accessed via www.findagrave.com on November 25, 2017.

15. Isaac H. Elliott, *History of the Thirty-Third Regiment Illinois Veteran Volunteer Infantry in the Civil War* (Gibson City, IL: 33rd Illinois Regimental Association, 1902), 25.

16. Earl J. Hess, *The Civil War in the West: Victory and Defeat from the Appalachians to the Mississippi* (Chapel Hill: University of North Carolina Press, 2012), 57–58; "Our Special Cairo Dispatches," *Cleveland Morning Leader*, April 12, 1862; "The Bombardment of Island No. 10," *Chicago Daily Tribune*, March 21, 1862; "From Island No. 10," *Green Mountain Freeman*, March 22, 1862; "Western Military Correspondence," *New Orleans Daily Crescent*, March 26, 1862.

17. "From General Pope's Column," *Chicago Daily Tribune*, April 12, 1862; Frank Moore, ed. *Rebellion Record: A Diary of American Events* (New York: G. P. Putnam, 1862), 4: 440; "The Result at Island 10," *Natchitoches Union*, May 8, 1862; "Tuesday, April 1," *New York Herald*, December 28, 1862; "Our Special Cairo Dispatches," *Cleveland Morning Leader*, April 19, 1862; *Naval OR*, ser. 1, vol. 22: 757; Rear Admiral H. Walke, *Naval Scenes and Reminiscences of the Civil War in the United States, on the Southern and Western Waters* (New York: F. R. Reed 1877), 153. In addition to the *Ohio Belle*, Union forces captured or destroyed several other boats at Island No. 10, including the *DeSoto, Yazoo, Red Rover, Simonds, Admiral, Mars, Grampus, Mohawk,* and *Winchester. OR*, 22: 757.

18. "US Senate Report to Accompany Bill S855," *Reports of Committees of the Senate,* 1–2.

19. "US Senate Report to Accompany Bill S855," *Reports of Committees of the Senate,* 1–2; "Our Mississippi River Correspondence," *New York Herald*, April 18, 1862; *OR*, vol. 17, pt. 1: 147; "Our Special Cairo Dispatches," *Cleveland Morning Leader*, April 12, 1862; *Naval OR,* ser. 1, vol. 23: 691; A Committee of the Regiment, *The Story of the Fifty-Fifth Regiment Illinois Volunteer Infantry in the Civil War* (Clinton, MA: W. J. Coulter, 1887): 270.

20. W. A. Wash, *Camp, Field, and Prison Life* (St. Louis, Southwestern Book and Publishing, 1870), 63; "From the 58th Illinois Regiment—Letter from One of the 'Tribune' Soldier Boys," *Chicago Tribune*, February 22, 1865.

21. *Roster and Record of Iowa Soldiers in the War of the Rebellion* (Des Moines, IA: Emory H. English, 1910), 3: 1652, 330; J. T. Woods, *Services of*

the Ninety-Sixth Ohio Volunteers (Toledo, OH: Blade Printing and Paper, 1874), 213; Homer B. Sprague, *History of the 13th Infantry Regiment of Connecticut Volunteers During the Great Rebellion* (Hartford: Case, Lockwood, 1867), 189; Wash, *Camp, Field, and Prison Life*, 65.

22. *Opening of the Mississippi, or Two Years Campaigning in the South-West* (Madison, WI: William J. Park, 1864), 87.

23. William Jewett Tenney, *The Military and Naval History of the Rebellion in the United States* (New York: D. Appleton, 1865): 189; Benjamin Franklin Cooling, *Fort Donelson's Legacy: War and Society in Kentucky and Tennessee, 1862–1863* (Knoxville: University of Tennessee Press, 1997), 110; "Letter from Memphis," *Chicago Daily Tribune*, September 30, 1862; "Daring Attempt to Capture the Steamer Eugene at Randolph, Tenn.," *The Daily Evansville Journal*, September 29, 1862; "Army Correspondence: Letter from the 46th Regiment," *Weekly Lancaster Gazette*, October 9, 1862.

24. "Our Memphis Letter," *Chicago Daily Tribune*, November 11, 1862; "From Cairo and Below," *Chicago Daily Tribune*, November 26, 1862; *OR*, vol. 17, pt. 1: 614; *Naval OR*, ser. 1, vol. 23: 563.

25. Virgil Carrington Jones, "U.S.S. Tyler," in Faust, ed. *Historical Times Illustrated Encyclopedia of the Civil War*, 768; Jack Myers, "USS Tyler," *The Encyclopedia of Arkansas History and Culture*, accessed online from http://www.encyclopediaofarkansas.net/encyclopedia/entry-detail .aspx?entryID=7726 on January 2, 2018; *Naval OR*, ser. 1, vol. 23: 216.

26. *OR*, vol. 3: 152, 200.

27. *OR*, vol. 3, 271, 276.

28. *OR*, vol. 7: 122, 153, 154, 421; *Naval OR*, ser. 1, vol. 23: 77.

29. *Naval OR*, ser. 1, vol. 23: 90; Kenneth P. Williams, *Grant Rises in the West: The First Year, 1861–1862* (Lincoln: University of Nebraska Press, 1997), 381; Steven E. Woodworth, *Nothing But Victory: The Army of the Tennessee, 1861–1865* (New York: Alfred A. Knopf, 2005), 190; Larry J. Daniel, *Shiloh: The Battle that Changed the Civil War* (New York: Simon and Schuster, 1997), 265; James Lee McDonough, *Shiloh: In Hell Before Night* (Knoxville: University of Tennessee Press, 1977), 173.

30. *OR*, vol. 15: 32; *Naval OR*, ser. 1, vol. 23: 258; John Spurgeon, "CSS Arkansas," *The Encyclopedia of Arkansas History and Culture*, accessed from http://www.encyclopediaofarkansas.net/encyclopedia/entry-detail.aspx?entryID=2854 on January 2, 2018.

31. *Naval OR*, ser. 1, vol. 23: 685, 686; David J. Eicher, *The Longest Night: A Military History of the Civil War* (New York: Simon and Schuster, 2001), 304.

Notes

32. *OR,* vol. 19: 38 ("Pilots Sebastian . . ."), 39, 40 ("behaved in the most cowardly . . ."); "Miscellaneous," *Memphis Public Ledger,* July 14, 1876; "Local Brevities," *Cincinnati Daily Star,* July 12, 1876.

33. Isaac N. Brown, "The Confederate Gun-Boat 'Arkansas,'" *Battles and Leaders of the Civil War* (New York: Century, 1888), 3: 574–575.

34. *OR,* vol. 15: 33; *Naval OR,* ser. 1, vol. 23: 680, 681, 672; Brown, "The Confederate Gun-Boat 'Arkansas,'" 575. A month after fighting the Union fleet, the *Arkansas* engaged the *Essex,* a Union vessel. During the battle, the engine of the *Arkansas* failed. Therefore, the crew set the *Arkansas* on fire and scuttled the gunboat to keep it out of Union hands. Spurgeon, "CSS Arkansas," *The Encyclopedia of Arkansas History and Culture.*

35. *Naval OR,* ser. 1, vol. 23: 244.

36. *Williams Cincinnati Directory, June 1863* (n.p., n.d., 1863), 310; *Cincinnati Enquirer,* February 15, 1863; Wash, *Camp, Field, and Prison Life,* 64–65.

37. "From Vicksburg," *Chicago Daily Tribune,* June 3, 1863; soldier and Earl J. Hess quoted in Earl J. Hess, *Civil War Logistics: A Study of Military Transport* (Baton Rouge: Louisiana State University Press, 2017), 59.

38. "From Memphis and Below," *Chicago Daily Tribune,* September 26, 1863; *OR,* vol. 30, pt. 3: 864.

39. "US Senate Report to Accompany Bill S855, *Reports of Committees of the Senate,* 1; "River News," *Evansville Daily Journal,* February 4, 1863; *Cincinnati Enquirer,* December 31, 1863; "River and Steamboat News," *Cincinnati Enquirer,* January 25, 1864; *OR,* vol. 34, pt. 2: 285. Federal authorities had to approve some of the *Belle'*s trade along the Ohio River. Wartime restrictions existed to keep goods out of rebel hands. Cooling, *To the Battles of Franklin and Nashville and Beyond,* 255–256. Berry Craig writes, "Louisville was the only port on the south bank of the Ohio in Kentucky where cargo could be shipped without a permit." Barry Craig, *Kentucky Confederates: Secession, Civil War, and the Jackson Purchase* (Lexington: University Press of Kentucky, 2014), 186 (quote), for trade restrictions, see 186–187.

40. "From Cairo and Below," *Chicago Daily Tribune,* March 30, 1864; "Guerrilla Amusement," *Evansville Daily Journal,* May 3, 1864.

41. "The Red River Expedition," *The Smoky Hill and Republican Union,* April 30, 1864; "The Red River Expedition—Two Giant Battles," *Indiana State Sentinel,* May 2, 1864; "The Red River Expedition," *Dayton Daily Empire,* April 25, 1864; J. W. Vance, *Report of the Adjutant General of the State of Illinois* (Springfield, IL: H. W. Rokker, 1886), 5: 240; *OR,* vol. 41, pt. 3: 41.

42. *OR,* series 2, vol. 8: 487; *OR,* vol. 48, pt. 2: 768.

43. *Cincinnati Enquirer*, December 18, 1865; *Cincinnati Enquirer*, March 31, 1866. The *Belle* was advertised to be sold by the Federal government in August 1865, which indicates the vessel had been sold to Union authorities. "Proposals," *Nashville Daily Union*, August 20, 1865.

8. A High Sense of Truth and Honor

1. "Camille," *New Orleans Daily Crescent*, March 24, 1856; "Miss Matilda Heron in Medea," *New York Times*, March 17, 1857; David Williamson, *The 47th Indiana Volunteer Infantry: A Civil War History* (Jefferson, NC: McFarland, 2012), 76; Humble, "Heron," *Notable American Women*, 1: 188.

2. "Mississippi," *Memphis Daily Appeal*, January 15, 1872; "Holly Springs, Miss.," *Memphis Daily Appeal*, January 16, 1888; "Railway Accident," *Memphis Daily Appeal*, September 29, 1874; "Holly Springs, Miss.," *Memphis Daily Appeal*, November 23, 1884.

3. *Cincinnati Enquirer*, April 6, 1866, 4; *Cincinnati Enquirer*, April 7, 1866: 4; "Death of Capt. John Sebastian," *The Emporia News*, July 14, 1876; *Williams Cincinnati Directory, June 1866* (Cincinnati: Cincinnati Directory Office, 1866): 375; "Gleanings from Our Exchanges," *Evansville Journal*, June 27, 1867.

4. "Death of Capt. John Sebastian," *The Emporia News*, July 14, 1876; "Nomination in Hamilton County," *Daily Ohio Statesman*, August 29, 1867; "Gleanings from Our Exchanges," *Evansville Journal*, August 30, 1867; "River News," *Louisville Daily Courier*, August 30, 1867; "Telegraphic News," *Louisville Daily Journal*, October 14, 1867.

5. "Death of Capt. John Sebastian," *The Emporia News*, July 14, 1876; "News and Editorial Items," *The Emporia News*, November 25, 1870; "Local Brevities," *Cincinnati Daily Star*, July 12, 1876; 1875 Census, Emporia, Lyon County, Kansas, Kansas State Census Collection, 1855–1925, accessed via Ancestry.com on September 17, 2017; "The Toughest Town," *The Phillipsburg Herald*, January 2, 1896.

6. "Disastrous Fire," *The Emporia News*, March 22, 1872.

7. "Local Brevities," *Cincinnati Daily Star*, October 12, 1875; "Death of Capt. John Sebastian," *The Emporia News*, July 14, 1876.

8. "Driftwood," *Louisville Courier-Journal*, July 14, 1876; "Miscellaneous," *Memphis Public Ledger*, July 14, 1876; "Death of Capt. John Sebastian," *The Emporia News*, July 14, 1876; "Local Brevities," *Cincinnati Daily Star*, July 12, 1876; "Capt. John Sebastian," Memorial #17989982, FindAGrave.com, accessed September 17, 2017.

9. "Report of Steam Navigation," *Report on the Agencies of Transportation*, 13; Hubbard and Taulbee, *Kentucky's Ohio River Boundary*, 24; Gould, *Fifty Years on the Mississippi*, 369. For the decline of steamboats, see Hunter, *Steamboats on the Western Rivers*, 484–495.

10. "Proposals," *Nashville Daily Union*, August 20, 1865; "River News," *Louisville Daily Courier*, October 11, 1866; "Sale of Boats at New Orleans," *Louisville Daily Courier*, January 11, 1866; "Report of the Secretary of War," *Executive Documents Printed By Order of the House of Representatives, During the Second Session of the Thirty-Ninth Congress, 1866–1867* (Washington, DC: US Government Printing Office, 1867), 188.

11. Captain Frederick Way Jr., "River Namesakes of the State of Ohio," *Ohio Archaeological and History Quarterly* 60 (1951): 283; "Steamboats," *New Orleans Daily Crescent*, February 3, 1866; "Steamers Leaving This Day," *New Orleans Daily Crescent*, March 27, 1866; "Marine Intelligence," *New Orleans Daily Crescent*, February 5, 1866.

12. "Alabama Belle," *New Orleans Times-Picayune*, September 20, 1866.

13. Wyllie, *Confederate States Navy*, 171; Early and Early, *Ohio Confederate Connection*, 195; "Ships of the Confederate States: CSS Ohio Belle," Department of the Navy—Navy Historical Center, accessed via https://www.ibiblio.org/hyperwar/onlinelibrary/photos/sh-us-cs/csa-sh/csash-mr/ohio-bel.htm on September 17, 2017.

Conclusion

1. "Underground Railroad," *The Liberator*, March 7, 1856.

Index

Index

Cameron, R. A., 99

Camille (Dumas, trans. Heron), 6, 40, 100

Campbell County, Kentucky, 21, 22

Campbell County, Virginia, 72

Carondelet (Union gunboat), 94

Carter, Joseph, 48

Catahoula (steamboat), 92

Cave Hill Cemetery, Louisville, 46

Cave-in-Rock, Illinois, 44

C. E. Hillman (steamboat), 82

Chancellor (steamboat), 57

Chase, Salmon P., 25, 26, 27, 36, 81

Cincinnati (steamboat), 10

Cincinnati, Ohio, 70, 85; James G. Birney in, 25; businesses and manufacturing in, 30, 32; and construction of *Ohio Belle*, 17, 20; and construction of *Sultana*, 15; as departure point for *Ohio Belle*, 19, 81, 98; as departure point for other vessels, 35, 46, 47, 99; Margaret Garner in, 35; growth of, 30–31; Matilda Heron performs, 40; as home of John Sebastian, 34, 96, 101; and Kentucky slaves, 22; *Ohio Belle* based in, 32; *Ohio Belle* deliveries, 80; and population, 13, 21; pork processing in, 31, 32; river workers riot, 58; Charles Sebastian attacked, 45–46; secessionist weapons seized, 83, 84; Spring Grove Cemetery in, 64; as steamboat center, 31–32; and steamboat construction, 10, 13, 32; steamboats in, 30, 31; and steamboat traffic, 11, 13; Stevens's body shipped there and funeral,

64; Alexis de Tocqueville on, 30, 104; and Watson-Hoppess case, 23, 27

Cincinnati and New Orleans Express Packet Line, 79, 80

City Belle (steamboat), 46

Civil War, US, 25, 26, 107; actions of *A. O. Tyler*, 93–96; Arkansas governor orders seizure of northern steamboats, 83; Arkansas plantation burned, 92; attack on Helena, Arkansas, 92; Battle of Belmont, 93; Battle of Shiloh, 93; burning of Randolph, Tennessee, 91; Confederate service of the *Ohio Belle*, 86–88; description of *A. O. Tyler*, 92; Fort Donelson, 93; Fort Henry, 93; Fort Sumter, 82; guerrilla violence, 90, 91, 98; Island No. 10, 88; Lincoln calls for 75,000 troops, 82; Mississippi River blocked, 82; *Ohio Belle* seized, 84; operations around Vicksburg, 97; Red River campaign, 98; secessionists attack *Westmoreland*, 85; states secede, 82; steamboats seized, 82, 85, 86; trade between North and South, 81–82; Union engagement against the *Arkansas*, 94–96; Union service of the *Ohio Belle*, 90–92, 96–99; wartime damage to Napoleon, Arkansas, 86; weapons seized at Cairo, Illinois, 82; weapons seized at Cincinnati, 83

class prejudice affecting media coverage, 72

Cleburne, Patrick, 87

144

Index

Index